© 1972, 2007 by Stephen Gaskin

Cover design: Warren Jefferson
Interior design: Gwynelle Dismukes
Photo: male orangutan (#312709) © American Museum of Natural History

Published in the United States by
Book Publishing Company
P.O. Box 99
Summertown, TN 38483
1-888-260-8458

Printed in Canada

ISBN 978-1-57067-195-1

13  12  11  10  09  08  07          7  6  5  4  3  2  1

Gaskin, Stephen.
  The caravan / by Stephen Gaskin. -- Rev. ed.
    p. cm.
  ISBN 978-1-57067-195-1
  1.  Gaskin, Stephen--Travel--United States. 2.  United States--Description and
travel. 3.  Spiritual life. I. Title.

  BP610.G3713 2007
  204--dc22
                        2006100271

---

The Book Publishing Co. is a member of Green Press Initiative. We have elected
to print this title on paper with 100% postconsumer recycled content and
processed chlorine free, which saved the following natural resources:

29 trees
21 million BTUs
2,588 bs of greenhouse gases
10,741 gallons of wastewater
1,379 lbs of solid waste

For more information visit: www.greenpressinitiative.org.
Savings calculations thanks to the Environmental Defense Paper Calculator at
www.papercalculator.org

# The Caravan

## Revised Edition

## by Stephen Gaskin

Book Publishing Company
Summertown, Tennessee

*Obeisance to the Guru*

# *Foreword*

*It's been fun writing this new version of* The Caravan. *The first edition contained only the speaking engagements and had no exposition at all. In this one, I've put in some stories of what happened to us on the road seven or eight, nine thousand miles around the United States.*

*And, as far as the text goes, mostly what I've tried to do is make it so it works better in the present day. I've decided not to account for every single thing I took out as I did in my annotations of* Monday Night Class. *But I took out repetitions, stuff that didn't work, and stuff that was dumb that I didn't want to add to the world.*

*Other than that, it's pretty much the way it came. It's been a lot of fun remembering the stories of what happened to us on the road.*

*Stephen*

---

EDITOR'S NOTE: *In this new edition of* The Caravan, *we have included some of the original photos and also some new ones; we have tried to place photos where they make the most sense.*

*About the different typestyles:* Stephen's original words appear in serif type like this.

*Stories about what happened along the Caravan are indented in italic, sans serif type.*

[Stephen's annotations and remarks from today's perspective are bracketed in plain sans serif type or boxed in gray.]

# Introduction

The genesis of the Caravan was really when a group of preachers from all over the United States came to San Francisco to study the hippies.

In San Francisco we had been doing this large meeting called Monday Night Class for about five years. All kinds of people came, but I have to admit most of them were hippies. There were old people and retired people, college dropouts as well as graduates, and a generous sprinkling of ethnic and religious diversity. There were Vietnam vets as well as war protesters and some who were both.

We started being together in a spiritual community on a love and trust basis and being peaceful and pretty happy and pretty healthy and pretty sane, physically healthy and good-looking, a good healthy monkey place.

The preachers who came to study the hippies were addressed by cops and social workers and psychiatrists, and I was the only hippy who got to speak with them. I told them that actually what we were having was a spiritual event, that they were in the right business and they didn't have to change business. I told them the idealistic view of hippies I carried, they liked me and they went back and set me up on a speaking tour in all their home churches all around the United States. And that's what started us on the Caravan. I spoke in 42 states on the Caravan.

When I was asked to go on the tour, I was already living in a schoolbus. It just seemed logical to go in the bus. Many people wanted to come on the road trip with me, so I said they had to get their own buses. We went out around the United States, going first to Washington State to speak.

My first lesson in leading something big that moved was when we left in the evening on Columbus Day, October 12, 1970, from The Family Dog on the Coast Highway in San Francisco. I got up almost to the Golden

Gate Bridge and looked in the rearview mirror, and there weren't any buses behind me.

I turned around, went back to where I lost them, and proceeded at a much more sedate pace, as one must when one is leading a caravan of 25 school buses.

Our first real idea of what it was like to be on the road came at a rest stop just inside California, almost up to Oregon, where we were going to stay for the night. A policeman came in his car, and he said, "I'm sorry, you can't stay here. You'll have to move on."

I said, "Well, we're just stopping for the night. It's kind of late to keep driving."

"No, you're going to have to move right on."

I knew he was doing something to us but I didn't know what, so we moved right on. When we crossed the line into Oregon, the full horizon erupted in red, white, and blue lights, and there were sheriffs and cops and county mounties and city kitties and all the different kinds of cops there are.

They stopped us all and they checked us out, and then one of them came into our bus and said, "All right, we've got orders to arrest the registered owner of this bus."

And my friend Michael, whose bus it was, said, "What!?" because it was obvious that they wanted me.

They came back in about an hour and said, "Well, actually, who we're supposed to arrest is Stephen Gaskin."

They arrested me and took me and put me in the jail up in Grants Pass, Oregon. And the Caravan went out and parked and came in to make my bail. The cops were embarrassed when the hippies made my bail with a great messy pile of ones and fives and a huge pile of change.

We had to go in front of the judge, and we told the judge what we were doing, said we were the peaceful hippies and we were about peace, and we were on a national tour about peace.

And he said, "Well, I'll tell you what I'm going to do. You go ahead, make your speaking engagements, and then you come back here and we'll look and see what you were, and then we'll know what to do about you."

ometimes I think the fall of man was learning to talk. It isn't necessary to either write or talk to become enlightened. Especially not to read or write … and not even necessary to talk.

I don't punch anybody's ticket. Everybody knows that I just don't do that. We don't want to be a hierarchical scene. Usually the only person I ever say that I saw that was really outstanding is a Zen master in San Francisco named Suzuki Roshi. Purest mind I ever saw. But I saw another mind, I have to say, quite similar to his one night in class.

People were gathering, and there were only a couple of hundred people. It was pretty early and the class wasn't full yet. And a little girl got up on stage—about toddler size. She made little singing noises that were pretty pleasant, and then she clapped her hands, and everybody thought that was cute, and a bunch of people gave her a little bit of applause. So she sang another little song and they gave her some applause. I watched the transaction happen, and it wasn't the usual kind of ego trip that kids get on. Usually a kid doing that is just ripping off everybody in sight, but this little girl wasn't doing that, she was having a really heavy pure exchange with everybody.

I watched that happen and I was mind-blown by her, and someone said, "Who's that?" And I said, "Guest lecturer." She got off the stage, and later on in the evening I saw her with her parents and I said, "That's a far out little girl, what's her trip?"

And they said, "She's a Down's syndrome child." It seems that being a Down's syndrome child is good for your ego. On some levels they aren't considered to be very smart. But she was really fine and pure, and she was doing telepathic complicated energy exchanges that are not measured in Stanford-Binets. It's really subtle out there, and really fast and really beautiful, and she could do that part good....

*Our progress across the United States was amazing. The police took us at our word that we were peaceful. We were handed from the Oregon police on to the Washington police, and as we went across each state line, the police in those states would meet the police in the new state and tell them that we were peaceful and we were all right and we weren't planning to stop and we weren't taking welfare.*

*And the police in the new town would take us at our word. And sometimes they would try to be cool and say something cool to us, like one of them said, "Let it be," letting us know in code, you know, like the Beatles say, "Let it be."*

*Another cop was more practical. He said, "As long as you guys stay in your buses and don't come bouncing down out of that bus with a joint in your mouth, we'll get along okay. Y'hear now?"*

SUNDAY MORNING SERVICE
REST STOP I-94, NORTH DAKOTA
25 OCTOBER 1970

Back there somewhere in the last state there was a National Grassland we passed through. Come on around and circle up closer if you want to. Nice windbreaker, too. When we passed through that National Grassland I thought for a second, What a funny thing, and then I thought, Well, you know, in California we're used to National Forests, they're all over the place. We've been through a bunch of National Forests on the way here already. I think Theodore Roosevelt liked that land and asked that it be saved. And when I was thinking about that this morning, the wind and this grass here made me realize that this grass has Spirit in it just like the trees; this grass is just as alive.

When I look at this grass out here and listen to it talk to us this morning, there's that place where when you think about it, it'll get stronger, and you think, Wow, it's getting stronger, and it gets stronger. And I see that Spirit is around us wherever we go.

We've been halfway across the continent and we're surrounded with it and we have the other half of the continent to go across. I was thinking of inside and outside, and as above so below, that what goes on inside of you is the same as what you make go on outside of you, and that everything that we manifest at the level of us here on the Caravan—what is it, a hundred and fifty of us, two hundred maybe?—is a microcosm of all of mankind. So we're out here working it out for everybody as we're passing through.

So far we've been leaving a good clean trail behind us. I don't know if there is a whole lot to say. Here we are. I don't feel like stopping for a day on the road even if it's Sunday because I think we ought to go on to Minneapolis and have a few days for folks to try to get out and earn some gas money. But it being Sunday, what say we take a few hours for a good Sunday morning breakfast and cut out and make some miles today. I love you all. God Bless you. Good morning.

*One of the towns that gave us the best welcome on the trip was Anoka, Minnesota. The people in Anoka were very practical. It was amazing. We came in there with, by this time, 40 buses anyway, and they said, "Oh, well, you're going to need to know where the gas station is to get these all gassed up, you're going to need to find out where the drinking water is to fill your drinking water tanks, you're going to need to dump your holding tanks, going to need to know where to put out your trash, going to need to shop for groceries."*

*They just made us available to all the businesses in the town, which was very smart and very sweet on their part. We were no trouble whatsoever, and we gave them an unexpected financial boost that day. Always had a soft spot in my heart for Anoka, Minnesota.*

*Q: Now when you use the term* stoned, *is this a condition brought on by drugs—or not necessarily?*

Not necessarily. The word *stoned*, by the way, comes from the word *astonied*, which is the root of the word *astonished*. "He fell as one *astonied*."

I just got really stoned on one of these babies in here a little while ago. I've been having a relationship with this particular baby since she was born. How old is she? Five months? Yeah, I've been meditating with her for about five months, and she gets me high every time we relate. We really love each other a lot. We have a very close personal relationship which has developed over the last five months. I look in her eyes and I let her have the kind of energy that a grown man has, and she lets me have the kind of energy that a new baby has. It's a fair exchange ratio and it gets us both high, because I can carry heavier-duty things than she can, on a level, because I'm grosser and older. I can take that kind of stuff off her. And she gives me what she's got, which is just pure juice, and she stones me. I think that is related to the "Adoration of the Infant." Not just Jesus, but all of them.

As we cruised along from town to town from speaking engagement to speaking engagement, our means of taking care of ourselves became much more obvious, and we began to learn that we would have to take care of each other.

José Mundo got a pickup truck, put in gas and oil and tires and batteries and tools, and followed the Caravan and tried to be sure that no stragglers were lost.

José had one other duty which we were profoundly grateful for, that was possibly the most frightening one. He had in the back of his pickup truck a 55-gallon drum with a good tight snap-on cap. When the buckets in the buses got too full of poop and pee, the next time that we'd stop they'd empty their bucket into José's barrel. And when the barrel was full, José and a crew of guys would go off somewhere—we know not where—and find a place where they could bury that gigantic barrel of poo. For this, we say that José Mundo was one of our first real thunder yogis.

After I was turned toward Spirit, the first thing I found out that blew my mind was that telepathy was real. That was the first thing, because I began to feel other people's minds. Then I realized from that, that other stuff has got to be true, because religion is the wiring diagram of the way human energy is moved to relate with the universe. Now that tells about how come I'm here talking about this kind of thing at all. Now that we all know that …

By the way, folks, if you're stacking up at the door, there's a balcony up there. There's a door down at the end there that goes right up to the balcony. Scootch up as much as you can.

Now all of that brings us to here and now. We have found over a long period of time, that we can interact in such a way that we can all find out what we need to know … that as we sit here like this we're a group mind.

Now here's the thing about telepathy: Telepathy is people's electrical fields being able to sense each other. See, everyone has an electrical field surrounding him, because part of your equipment's electrical, and anything electrical has a field around it. We call that field an aura. You know, you see religious pictures with people with light around their heads and stuff? That's an aura. Also if you've taken some psychedelics you've probably seen auras.

And if two people's fields can merge in that fashion, then everybody's field can. One person's field overlaps with another's. It's not that you're there and your field comes out like this. Your field is large enough to fill this room. So think that each person here's field is large enough to fill up this whole room, and that we have this many people's electrical energy superimposed, one on top of the other. There's a pretty strong fabric of consciousness here.

What I'd like to do is talk with you, because we drove all the way here to talk with you. So I'd like questions about anything—Spirit, religion, sex, dope, birth, marriage, what have you.

*Q: How was the weather on the way from California?*

It started snowing in Yellowstone just after we left, and it snowed a great deal, and it's been snowing just as we leave everywhere we go, all the way here. We're running just ahead of it. It's cool. We've got the snow just behind us and five hundred miles of good police teletype in front of us. They like us. They send word down the line that we're cool.

There was one other little thing that the park police had to say to us while we were there in Yellowstone. One of them said, "You probably ought to be getting on down the road. We know you're all right, but we have to tell you that ever since Charlie Manson got a little weird, some of your longhaired people ate somebody a little ways down the road there. So you guys just be good, and you'll be okay."

Some Minneapolis police came into the parking lot yesterday, said they'd just heard about us in the paper and wanted to come talk to us. I can see where they were at—usually to talk to a beatnik they have to bust him. It's the only way they can get one around them for long enough to talk to him. But they just came out to talk to us, and one of them said he felt like taking off his coat and badge and getting a school bus and joining the Caravan, and as they left, the other one said, "Maybe we'll go refinance our houses and get school buses." One of them kept saying, "It's like Huck Finn, you know? It gets people's heads about doing a thing like that."

*Q: Is Minneapolis turned on?*

Yeah, Minneapolis is turned on. I think it's not just the long-hairs, the long-hairs are like family everywhere you go, and sometimes it's the same family because we swap around so much. But what gets me here in this city is the straight people are so honest. They're really clean.

And it's been that way since we started leaving big cities. I think the east coast and the west coast are in sort of last stages of Roman Empire, but out here in the middle it feels pretty sound. It really does.

*Q: Could you talk about living on love?*

Living on love? I don't know what you mean by living on love. Living in love I can see, living in love all the time … just be in love with everybody you see.

Love is a word that has a denotation, a real meaning, and that meaning is, when the electrical field between people is charged with their energy so that there's a high level of body telepathy between them, so that they can feel each other—that is being in love. That's the technical thing. It's really real, and you can tell.

I know people that to just walk up and stand beside them turns me on, makes me feel good. They have a strong compassion thing, a lot of love. I really do a lot of love with those folks. We're doing a lot of love here. For this many of us to be this close together and this groovy puts out a pretty strong field. Living in love I think is just meeting everybody you meet straight on.

As an individual human being has a field, humankind has a field, and an individual human being's field can be called their soul. See, you've got body, soul and Spirit, not just two, but three, and the soul is the electrical part surrounding you, and there's an electrical part surrounding all of humankind too, and that's the soul of humankind. That's the matrix, that's the tapioca pudding that we're all tapiocas in. And then there's the Spirit, which is just—the one.

*Q: Would you talk about the revolution?*

I think that the revolution's been going on for, oh, maybe the last hundred thousand years, and during the last hundred thousand years people have figured out how it works. The object is to make everything better, right? The object of revolution is not to shoot anybody; the object of revolution is not to burn anything. Those things are maybe incidentals if you do a material-plane kind of revolution. The object is that it be groovy for everybody. Well, over the last fifty or a hundred thousand years we've figured out how hard can you push and in what direction to make it groovy for everybody, that will work and accomplish the goal.

The ground rules for revolution have been discovered to be that we must consider that everybody we have is necessary and that nobody is expendable … that killing any of us will not improve the lot of the survivors … and that it must be motivated directly out of love and selfless devotion. It cannot be for self. It cannot be to profit anybody. I think that the revolution that does include everybody and does assume that we need all of us to make it and that we can't say any of us are expendable has been going on and is going on, and this is some of it right here, and it's been going on for a long time.

*Q: Is it wrong to do head trips on people? Like you walk into a place where there's maybe twenty people and somebody starts messing with your head, or you start messing with somebody else's head … Is that wrong?*

Yes, things that you do mentally matter, and if you be kind of violent in your head it's like being violent with your bod, it's not any different.

Psychic violence is just like physical violence, and if you find that you can't have any communication with anybody's head, the thing to do is to start establishing communication and learn to get a little love happening. Every little bit helps.

It is also okay when you and your friends get in a good mind place to play with it and enjoy it and learn from it.

*Q: Does that mean a decision on the psychic plane, where you decide whether it's going to be physical or not? Like you can be astrally violent, but you have a decision to make, whether to bring that out on the physical plane.*

What happens is, if you be psychically violent long enough, sooner or later it'll get into physical. Whatever you keep running through your head, over and over again, will sooner or later manifest. That's what causes what they call the obsessive-compulsive cycle, where somebody gets afraid something's going to happen, then spends so much time thinking about it that it happens. You just have to stop it at the level of thought. You can't have the violence in your head, because it will out. It will come out and make things happen.

*Q: Do you think the best kind of learning comes from actual experience like your travels on the road?*

The only kind of learning comes from actual experience. My oldest girl, at about two years old, walked up to a candle and looked at it very curiously for a long time, and she put up her hand and I knew she was going to touch it, and I had an impulse to say, "Don't touch it." Then I thought, I'll keep my mouth shut and see what happens.

It didn't hurt her. She saw what it was quick enough to get back out of it, but she never touched it again either. And the word that meant fire-flame in her head had a referent that came in from another sense and was cross-indexed. It really meant something. If I had stopped her before she touched it, then the word fire would have had a referent of, "Last time I tried to do anything about it they said don't do it."

We're pretty durable, and we need to bump up against the universe a little bit to find out where it's at. Also we need to bump up against each other a little bit. We shouldn't think that we're so fragile that we can't lean on each other a little bit and interact kind of heavy and still be friends.

Getting away from the small village idea has done a funny thing to the whole country, because in a small village, if a fellow turns up obnoxious one day he's still going to be living there the next day, and he's either going to have to straighten up or nobody's going to talk to him anymore or something. He's going to get cooled.

But here in the city you can get obnoxious and move to another neighborhood, and get obnoxious and move to another neighborhood … and people get the idea that if you're going to have to come on heavy to somebody to make them straighten up that they might not like you anymore, and they might move, and you'd never see them again or something. But we should all think that we're all good enough friends—we're all kind of like cousins anyway, we're all the same kind of monkey—that we can say, "Hey, man, how about it," once in a while, and the other fellow isn't necessarily going to say, "Well, I'm going to go home."

That's another part of interacting, getting into that learning experience. We learn how we be by bumping against each other a little bit, and it's a good deal all the way around to have a learning experience. We've really learned a lot on the road, too. One thing I learned … I said in my book [*Monday Night Class*] that the country was so corrupt that it was falling down, which is what it looks like from San Francisco. But it looks a lot solider out here. It looks a lot solider. It looks like these folks would be easier to make friends with than to do anything else.

*Q: About compassion and politics … if you go mess up a draft board, is that being compassionate for one's brother?*

No, if you go in and tear up somebody's thing, it's going to blow their mind and wreck their head, and that means that there's one more wrecked head that we've got to pick up, because we aren't going to be cool until we pick up all the wrecked heads—it doesn't matter whose they are. We can't be cool until we get everybody cool and sane. There's no final enlightenment until everybody can get off. You can only go so far, and then you've got to stop and help everybody get off, and that means everybody. So it's immoral to mess up folks' heads—anybody's. I try to leave everybody's head a little better than I found it; it doesn't matter who he be.

I will tell you the best way for your revolution to be successful: You have to run your revolution in such a way that you can win the love of an honest square.

People don't hurt people that they know well, so just make yourself know everybody well and let them know you well. Be wide open. Don't hide anything and don't act like you're superior to them a little bit or anything. Get right in there with them, and if you do that, they'll have compassion with you, and if they have compassion with you, they can't hurt you; they won't want to, they won't want to hurt anybody.

We make a lot of difference: There's a string of hundreds and hundreds of cops halfway across this continent who are well-disposed toward the next long-hair they meet, because the last two hundred of them they met were a groove. And we're going all the way around the country doing that—trying to get other folks to do it too, because if we can build enough individual human bonds of love and trust, we can raise the whole love-trust thing for the whole country and for the whole world, and it's really necessary that it be done.

We've come to such a good agreement that on a spontaneous feeling, I feel like cutting us loose. What time is it, does anybody know? Ten after twelve? Happy Halloween, it's now All Saints' Day. It's now the day of the Feast of All Saints. We waited out the watch, Halloween's over, and it's a groove, and here we are, and God Bless you all.

Now we're going to have a short drivers' meeting, if you don't mind. Highway 35 is about three blocks from here. The entrance to it? Somebody's going to scout that out and find out which direction. Why don't you; you've got a small truck. I'm not going to pull out of the parking lot until everybody's motor is running. The way I'm going to know if your motor's running is because your headlights and markers are all going to be on, right? So we're gonna stow and go, and God Bless you, Minneapolis, and thank you for letting us be here. Thank you all, and good night.

A lot of times when I'm doing a talking thing I have to start way back when I used to do something else, and then got turned on to Spirit, and then went through a bunch of changes which end up with us being here with you, which is now this large conglomerate *us*.

Now *us* must mean everybody. I can't talk about the establishment anymore. All I can talk about is our parents. Calling them the establishment puts them in a place of calling us the anti-establishment. I'd rather call them our parents and cop that we're their kids. They're getting old, and they're afraid that we're too dumb to take over the show.

A couple of old men in a yellow truck stopped to look at our Caravan. They were Minnesota Highway Department, built the highways. Learned a lot of things from folks like that, talked about old Charlie Babcock, father of the modern highway system. They were really neat.

They came into our bus and they said, "Like to look at your bus, ha-ha, gonna check out your workmanship, ha-ha-ha." And they came on in and they checked out our workmanship.

They wanted to see was it made out of papier-mâché and psychedelic paint or would it keep the rain out. The only reason they're afraid about psychedelics is they're afraid that they make you untogether, because so many of us have been so conspicuously untogether since we've been taking them.

I think the Spirit's rampant in this country ... around the world, but in this country because this country's like a hothouse for it. Because out there's the carnival, and remember, *carne* means meat. The carnival is bright lights and war and death and television and high prices and fancy consumer goods and planned obsolescence and all the rest of that trip, and that thing is so cumbersome and so clumsy that it's scaring the folks that have it.

They're beginning to notice the rivers tasting funny, and they're also getting old and know that somebody's going to take that stuff over, and they wonder if the man that's going to take that stuff over is competent. I know what the man at the rest stop out in Anoka, Minnesota, would want to know. He'd want to know would somebody turn off the water in the water fountain out in front of the rest stop every night so it wouldn't freeze and split the pipes, so there would be water for the travelers in the morning. That's what he would be concerned about. Because that's what he was concerned about when we were there.

I feel like beatniks have been spaced long enough, and that we know where it's at, and that it's time we got off welfare, gave up food stamps, and began to produce with this energy which we say we have so much of. They don't deny that we have a lot of juice. They just think it's a little strange to see people taking baths in energy while there's other people dying for lack of it. That's why they think we're funny about the way we use energy.

Understanding that you're one with all mankind means not only breaking down space barriers, in that you're one with people on the other side of the world and other countries and other planets and your next-door neighbor, but time barriers, in that you have to realize you are one with all people and with all people that will be and that it matters what we do. The universe comes down positive and negative, half and half, but the way in which you arrange it is up to you. You're an artist, and that's your work of art, how you arrange how the positive and the negative comes down in your life.

Enlightenment is not complicated. Everybody really knows where it's at. The only reason that all of us don't do it all of the time is because it's hard and you have to try. But you can, and everybody knows how. All you have to do is come up on top and tell the truth all the time. There's only the sudden school. If you spend twenty years trying to get enlightened, then you've been slow in the sudden school. There is no gradual school.

I'd like to do questions right now, and dialogue, and get into a conversation with the folks from Iowa City and everybody. Anything that we need to talk about … thinking on the sort system of this is a meeting of the monkeys, and when this many monkeys come together for a reason, and it is for a reason, folks want to know what to do. Questions like that are probably good.

*Q: What do you know of God?*

Ah ha, I would feel better if I could use my own definition. I don't believe God is a white-bearded old man in a long white nightdress, but the entire universe.

The way was made open for us because we were peaceful. People come up to us, like a fellow in Minneapolis, the inspector for the city, who came up to me to throw us out. The way this incident worked out is an example of the workings of God. He had been told to throw us out by his superior, and he was sent out after business hours for no other purpose than to do that. He came to see us to do that, and we talked a little bit and he didn't want to do that anymore.

I watched that fellow come up when his heart was hard, and I watched his heart soften. Even when I see people who are screwed up, I see the workings of karma, and I see that they're a part of the universe.

Everywhere I look, I see nothing out of order. When I say out of order, I mean nothing outside of the laws of cause and effect. There are things which I think we can do better than, like war and whatnot. We can do better than that. It's not worthy of monkeys to be doing that.

But I see nothing out of order. Which is very fine—it means it's all working according to the laws. That means that you can learn the laws and you can run the universe. That's how we're supposed to make it. We're not supposed to have to hassle each other about how we divide it up.

*Q: What is karma?*

Karma is the law of cause and effect. Now it works like this: Karma is like leverage. On the material plane there are laws about leverage, like you push down this side with a fulcrum in the middle and something comes up on this side, and how far you slide it back and forth makes a difference. And then they have the laws of hydraulics, which turns out to be the laws of leverage again, only working through liquids. Then they have the laws of electricity, which are the laws of leverage again but running through an electrical mode, and Boyle's law of gaseous expansion and all that is leverage again.

So the whole material plane comes down to being leverage finally, and leverage is nothing but cause and effect. Push down on this and it causes that to go up. That's all leverage is, is cause and effect. So cause and effect continues through the entire material plane and on into the spiritual planes.

That means that not only does your pushing down on a lever make a direct effect happen on the other end, but the way you be to somebody makes a direct effect happen on the other end, and you create your universe out in front of you by the way you run your end of the levers.

Now people say, "You hear about innocent little kids getting wasted, what kind of karma is that?"

Here's the thing about karma: Karma is not about deserving; karma's about cause and effect. And if a puppy runs in front of a truck and gets wasted for it, it's hard to say that a puppy gets wasted for being dumb enough to go in the street. It's a hard thing to say that. But it is most definitely cause and effect.

Well, cause and effect is how everything works. That's the name of the interaction. And that's karma. So good karma means that you've been doing good enough for a long enough string that your odds are very good that you're going to continue doing good, because things are working for you and you've got good cause and effect stacked up.

Q: *In the* I Ching *it talks about synchronicity, and I'm confused about…*

Cause and effect and synchronicity? Does that hang you up?

Q: *Yes.*

Okay. Cause and effect is not only a function of the material plane. It goes on through to the astral plane a lot, but in the highest spiritual plane there's not cause and effect, there's just cause … and all this is effect. Synchronicity is a description of the nature of the communication of the astral plane.

Now the astral plane is spaceless and timeless. That's what they say: the Kingdom is eternal … spaceless and timeless. That means that if you understand Socrates right now, it doesn't matter that he was then and you are now. You and him are right there together on that thought plane, because when he thought that, he made it timeless, and when you thought it and knew it with him, you got timeless too, and then you're both timeless.

If you speak Buddha's thoughts, then you are Buddha. That doesn't mean that you can play a tape-recording of Buddha and be Buddha. It means that if you come on to a situation and you have to work it out, and the way you work it out is like Buddha worked it out, and you come to the same conclusions through working it out and say the same thing, you're being Buddha while you're doing that ... although Gautama Buddha lived twenty-five hundred years ago and you live now.

Because it's synchronous—same time, right now, here and now in the astral plane, and that there was a Jesus ever means that there always is one. That there was a Buddha ever means there always is one. Sometimes I say, You seen one Buddha, you've seen 'em all.

*Q: What is Buddha like when he is like you and you are synchronous?*

Just like me when he's like me. Just like you when he's like you. Are you hip that the basic unit of time has the same laws as eternity does? Like the kronon is the still picture of time. Within the kronon you may not discern past, present or future, or cause and effect, same as eternity. But our experience as we perceive it with our finite mind is a function of space/time, and our infinite mind is not a function of space/time, and is a continuum or differential that goes from thing to no-thing. When we're on the thing end, we obey thing laws, and when we're on the no-thing end, we obey no-thing laws. No-thing laws have neat things in them like no inertia, which enable full-speed 90-degree flying-saucer-type turns, for example. That feels pretty stoned, but ... how are you doing? That cover you?

*Q: I think I'm on time.*

Hang in there. The first time I ever found out what death and rebirth as per the psychedelic experience was, was a realization about time.

I was in one of those places where I was holding ego and knew it, and knew that the end was imminent. I was afraid of the people I was with and didn't want to do it with them, and wanted to do it somewhere else, one of those trips … I ran around on this mountain-top and it rained and I was weird. I finally got in the front seat of my Metro truck, which was homelike enough to me that I thought I could do it there, so I looked around and nobody was looking and I just curled up there, me and the steering wheel and the speedometer, and let go.

And when I let go I saw time split, kronon from kronon, and I realized that with the positive and negative of existence, you don't have to worry about the negative part, because it isn't, that being its nature. And there was a kronon still picture of me here, and then it split apart, and there was nothing in there, and then here was this other kronon still picture of me and I was different. And I said, Wow, this is a new incarnation, and that's a past life. And I saw myself die and be reborn, and then realized that each one of us dies and is reborn each kronon, which is why I'm a believer in the sudden school. It means that you can straighten up right now.

*Q: May I propose a paradox?*

I don't believe in those, but …

*Q: What does a chameleon see in the mirror?*

That depends on whether he's paranoid or not. If he isn't uptight he doesn't see anything. What else is happening?

*Q: The first time I spent a few minutes looking at Michael's mandala* [the one on both Monday Night Class *and this book cover*] *it seemed to take me to a place like what you just described, where it opened up and there was nothing, and I was wondering if that sounds straight to you, and if that's what mandalas are for, to be a vehicle for that kind of thing.*

Here's what I like about the mandala: They have fire engine contests, you know, and they have these old pump fire engines. They bring out the old fire engines and they pump them up as hard as they can pump them, and there's men that design nozzles for fire engine competitions. They design a nozzle that's going to make a clean stick, they call it. It means that the nozzle is so perfect that the water comes out with not even fluted sides or anything—it just comes out a straight shaft of water for a long time. That's how they can get a long distance with those. The mandala puts out a clean stick of energy to me, like you can just throw anything in it, whoosshh … and it comes out, sheeoow…. You can let it collect you. You can use it like a parabolic reflector to throw yourself back in your face till you notice you're there. That's a meditation. It'll work.

*Q: Would you explain about how the different axes intersect, where you're supposed to find yourself in the center of all these?*

Yes. They say that a Zen master has to resolve thirty-two dichotomies and carry them resolved with him. I didn't know what that was about for a long time, although I noticed that it seemed to be a heavy thing, because the *I Ching* is also thirty-two pairs of things, you know. Then I started seeing some continuums that I hadn't seen.

One of the first continuums that I had seen was *eros* and *logos* … eros being the body, compassion side, red color … logos being blue color, intellect and figuring it out—as in erotic and logical. Now you can take that continuum and balance yourself on it so that you use your life energy to keep your brain high enough so that you can be smart enough to keep your life energy intact and run a whole integrated thing. Then you can think of the compassion axis, which is sadistic or masochistic on its extremes. When you're not sadistic and you're not masochistic, then you're compassionate … when you neither want to hurt or be hurt but you feel what's there. You feel all, then you're balanced.

Think of space and time: The intersection of space and time is here and now. People can slide off the continuum and get out-of-register in their space/time. That's schizophrenia. Another continuum is male and female; for purposes of energy-moving I consider myself to be androgynous. I don't consider myself to be either male or female when I'm in the energy-moving business, because if I do consider myself to be one, then my subconscious is going to be the other one, and I don't want to make my subconscious be anything different from me, so I just say, Okay, I'll be both of them here in the middle … and let that energy pass.

The thing about the continuums is that you have to track them down and discover them to make them your own. You have to see a way that people be and then learn that that's a variable. Conservative and liberal on the material plane is one of those, and conservative and liberal in the subconscious is also one of those … also a continuum.

You can be stingy about material-plane things or you can be stingy about energy-plane things—and be a conservative on either one of those planes. It works out that if you're conservative about material-plane things then you probably let astral things go by pretty liberally, and if you're conservative about astral things then you might let your material plane get sloppy.

Did you ever run into somebody who was hypercritical and knew everything that was happening and seemed to have really good vision, except that their house was all sloppy and a mess around them and their stuff all fell apart? That's an astral conservative—being out there being conservative about the astral plane and letting the material plane come apart. Those are continuums. I'm not into telling you what the thirty-two of them are. You do it non-linearly. You learn that straight balances you on all of them, and you learn enough of them to start finding out where that homes into.

*Q: When you say, "As above so below," it doesn't jibe with what you said about being liberal on one plane and conservative on another?*

As above so below means that the overall quality of how you're doing is the same here as on all the planes and that if you aren't being cool here you aren't cool anywhere else. How you get straight is you get the consciousness straight and the subconsciousness will get straight with it. That's why you go for the Golden Mean, which is looking for the center of the continuums. Now, as above so below means that the situation overall is the same. It's much like what Suzuki says about, "If it's raining, don't bother walking fast, it's raining everywhere."

*Q: How can you tell what you want inside?*

Because everybody has inside a fair witness who cannot be bribed, and who always knows what's going on, and who always tells the truth, and anybody who is blowing it is overriding that fair witness and holding their hand over its mouth and gagging it while they're doing that.

*Q: What do you do when people want to talk about their hassles?*

That depends on whether it's something constructive that's going to end that particular hassle and get it over with. I'm not one to say that you shouldn't hassle. If it comes out that you're going to do a little thing right now and get it over with so you can go ahead, then do that. But if it's somebody that's just complaining … complaining gives you bad teeth, bad skin around your mouth, causes bad vibes, complaining can croak you. If people are complaining around you, you just hip them that it's complaining, and it isn't good for you. It just runs your energy backward.

*Q: I'm thinking of the compassion continuum, where you have the sadist and the masochist, and I'm curious as to how the sadist or the masochist sees the continuum, and how other people fit on it?*

How they see the continuum from where they are? I don't think that they see the continuum. There's a place inside the Great Pyramid in

Egypt where you can be down inside and you look outside this hole and you can see clear out through that rock to a star out there. But if you're not exactly lined up with that hole you don't even know the hole's there. That's like the closer you get to the center of a continuum the more you understand it, and the farther you are out on it the less you understand it.

On some of those continuums you can be conservative or liberal about each sense. You can be conservative or liberal about eye, about things you look at. Like if you see something ugly, does it offend you so bad you can hardly stand it? Do you have to cover it up or fix it or change it immediately, or can you look at something that's a mess for a long time and it doesn't bug you?

You can also be conservative or liberal in ear or touch, like my lady was more conservative about what she felt than me. I used to laugh at

her because every night she'd tear the bed down and sweep all the crumbs and stuff out of it. She'd say, "Bed cruddies! Ahhgghh!" She was very conservative about what touched her skin, and I'd wear heavy sweaters with no T-shirt and didn't care. We both came in from that and achieved compassion between us, but it was a trip for a while.

*Q: Do you feel that if you were confronted with a person who did not want to play fair, by your viewpoint, that you could talk to them?*

I do, so far all the time, right down the line. Just right up to date. There's folks that just flat don't dig me. I would rather that everybody liked me. I think that would be neat. But there's free will, and I can't run over anybody's free will who doesn't want to. I'll try to talk folks out of things, but the thing is that nobody has to be around me either, if they don't want to. If they don't like me, they don't have to come close up to me.

I find that if I let people be around me and be a hassle that they get to be a worse hassle and a worse hassle and get on a worse ego trip. If I just tell them where it's at, it may dynamite them for a minute, but they'll come back in a few hours or a day or something and tell me that they understand. And so I do that. If somebody really seems to be on a trip, I just say so. Folks that know me long enough just get used to it and say, "Oh all right," and treat me like I'm the speedometer or the gas gauge or something and don't get emotional about it.

*Q: I heard you say politics … In one sense, things are actually happening and we should respond to it.*

I think that the political people are coming on like, "Well, you guys tried a spiritual revolution and see where it got you. Now it's time for the guns."

Politics may be a nasty business, and they say it makes strange bedfellows, but there are two things that politics is superior to, and I'm pretty sure. One of them is armed revolution, and the other one is enduring tyranny.

I USED TO THINK THAT POLITICS, if used for settling any questions heavier than where to put the sidewalks, didn't make it … and is not a heavy enough vehicle for the agreement necessary to keep mankind together. Things have changed and I have learned more to where I see that politics is the only vehicle. We have only to look at the Middle East and Ireland to see that religion is not the vehicle to carry the necessary discussion on the worldwide scale.

What are we to say when a country that calls itself the only superpower in the world changes hands in a coup d'etat as it did in 2000 and nothing is ever said and it gets swept under the rug by the next election?

This current political situation is the worst I've ever seen, but that's only because of its pervasiveness, not because I've never seen it before.

I've seen crooked politicians. Influence peddling is what they used to call it; they'd bust people for that now and then. The government culture is contaminated and polluted, and so is the corporate culture. It's hard to say "gentlemen's agreement" except in the satirical tone that the old movie *Gentlemen's Agreement* was named, when the gentlemen's agreement was to keep Jews out of real estate. This is the same kind of gentlemen and the same kind of nasty agreement, too. They excuse each other.

Cronyism is where these guys knowing each other is a higher law than the Constitution or the statutes. And so there isn't really a government there for us to be loyal to or not, because there isn't a government there. It's a void. And we have to pay taxes into that void, in which they are completely dishonest and expedient.

I'm not an anarchist, because I care too much about what's going on, and I don't think things will work themselves out without some intelligent help. I might be a synarchist, who thinks that there's a synthesis, and a synergy, that also can be driven and used to fill up the space left by the people who have abdicated all Constitutional and moral authority, as our government has.

The thing for the young people that they have to really try to do, is to understand that this is not ordinary. This is a totally extraordinary situation that we are in. It is not supposed to be this way. And that they are justified in being strong political activists and, anybody they have any influence over, to hold his feet to the fire to try to make him do right. And this is okay for the young people to do that. And they need to know that they need to start doing it when they're young.

The thing about how we got into this mess is that you don't get into a mess like this without a lot of people agreeing to it. And that's the really bad part about it, is the people agreeing to it. And the more people have a wink and a nudge and don't help each other, not tell the truth, and like that, is bringing down the level of agreement of humankind to do that. And it's an awful bad thing to do, because the agreement of humankind is how we can quit blowing up Palestinian villages, if we had the agreement of humankind. That's the kind of stuff you can do if you have the agreement of humankind. And the agreement right now is, the Democrats and the Republicans have a truce on ethics things.

George Bush has committed treason on a massive scale and, under the rules of the country and all that kind of thing, there'd be justification in hanging him. But ... it's not going to happen because nobody's ever going to enforce all those rules that way, anyway. And, as much as I think that about George Bush, I do not think that he was complicit in the airplane crashing of the Twin Towers. I think that it is ignorant to believe that. Anyone who believes that in a serious way has got a big spot in their computer that isn't working. You've got to see the way of the world a little bit to realize how impossible it would be to hide a secret like that.

*Q: I'm not questioning whether your theory is good or not, your beliefs are good, I'm just wondering what good they'll do, say after you're dead, say over a period of time.*

I'm not worried over that piece of it except insofar as we be very just and very pure and honest in the here and now, so that nobody will be able to say bad things about us after we're gone. They'll have to say, "That was cool."

You see, I'm really only a front man for a vast international syndicate, and it's not only inter-national but inter-spacial and inter-chronological, which is to say folks have been doing this same thing all the time for a long time. There's always been a few folks who knew where it was at and a few folks who really didn't know where it was at and a whole bunch of folks who were a little confused—the normal bell curve of distribution. Sometimes in history you get a lot of folks knowing where it's at. We have a lot of people knowing where it's at, or the potential of it.

*Q: Do you believe that we're each separate spirits?*

I believe that we've got separate bodies and semi-separate souls and we have identical spirits. It's body, soul and Spirit that we're made of. Go ahead ...

*Q: Well, what reason do you think is it that we each have separate souls?*

Because it's the normal laws of field behavior. Your soul is the electrical field that surrounds your equipment, and your brain is a field generator, it's not just a hunk of meat with wiring in it. Your brain is not like an adding machine with gears in it and stuff, it's a field generator, and your finest thoughts are the plays of the field—how the field moves, not just the mechanical tracing inside here—and that field is your soul. Your spirit is a fraction of the all and is identical with all other fractions of the all and is exactly identical—the same. Souls differ insofar as they interpenetrate; our souls all interpenetrate.

*Q: If you get in a hassle and you're being honest, how do you get past that?*

You can't tell anybody you're cool; nobody believes that in words. All you have to do is be cool, and if you be cool, if you are cool, people will dig you and you can tell that. Also I think one of the heaviest things you can do is to assume the other person's goodwill. That's a really heavy piece of magic, because you can be in it up to your ears and if you can assume the other person's goodwill, he can have some goodwill, and then you can connect.

*Q: Do you believe that expression of feeling is important?*

Expression of feeling ... that's a two-part question. On one hand it is not healthy to be bottled up and unable to express oneself. On the other hand you can't have an idea of expression of feeling where you put out raw, angry, unsorted and unresolved subconscious for other people to deal with.

I think that if people are in interaction, and if there's anything inside that you have that you're not copping to, you're broadcasting it telepathically. If you're coming on meek and mild and sweet to somebody and you don't believe it, you don't be that way really, that's not how you really feel about them; what's coming through telepathically is pride and arrogance. That's that thing about the consciousness and the subconsciousness having a reciprocal relationship.

*Q: So how do you relate that to being peaceful towards people, say, if you don't feel peaceful?*

How I feel is one of the things that I can have some control over. I can report to somebody what they're doing to me without being violent about it. The reason you aren't supposed to be angry is like you're not supposed to throw matches out into the dry grass. It's the same reason, because if you be angry you put out anger vibes and the folks around you—anybody around you who doesn't believe in telepathy, for instance, which may be a bunch of folks—has to feel your anger vibe and has no choice but to identify it as their own, them not believing in telepathy. Somebody can throw an anger trip and get a whole bunch of folks angry around him. So that's not acceptable, obviously. That screws up the system for everybody.

*Q: I'm hung up on the question of the relativity of truth.*

Relativity of truth. The Fourteenth Dalai Lama said that there's relative truth and absolute truth and that relative truth deals with knowledge and absolute truth deals with wisdom. How's that? Help you any?

*Q: It's confusing. I'll give it to you from my point of view. I believe that truth exists, and I believe that each of us sees it from his point of view.*

I believe that, too. I also believe that you can become selfless and accept the truth, whatever it may be. It means that you have to want to know the truth more than anything else. You have to want to know the truth if the truth means you're full of shit, and if you can accept that, then you can know truth.

The reason that I react that way about the relative truth idea is because if you get on that train and ride it very far it has a train wreck. If you get into relative truth, you get into where you don't know what's happening any more.

On a level we could do this all night, but I have to drive sixty miles tonight and I feel like it's getting late for everybody. I'm really happy with our visit here. I got to meet some good people. And the things I said about your scene I only said because it looks like a living, vital thing, and I would like to see it go on living. When I talk about wanting it to be pure, like yes, I have high standards about things, I'm looking for purity. That's high standards. The thing about purity is like the thing about truth. You strive for pure and then you do however good you do. But you strike on out for pure.

God Bless all you people and thank you for coming here.

*By the time we got to our next gig at Northwestern in Illinois, one of the ladies on the Caravan who was due began to have her contractions. And while I was inside lecturing to the people at Northwestern, Ina May and the ladies were out with her, helping her have that baby. And I took a break in the middle and went out to see them, and after the break I was able to announce to the crowd that the baby was born in the parking lot and it's just fine, and the crowd gave this great applause for that. Probably an act that was hard to follow.*

NORTHWESTERN UNIVERSITY
EVANSTON, ILLINOIS
8 NOVEMBER 1970

I always like to start off with the OM because it's a conversation in which everybody can speak at the same time and all be heard at once. When we say OM, that demonstrates the weight of all the voices that are heard for the remainder of the evening. Any question that is asked is asked with the voice of the OM and any answer is answered with the voice of the OM.

We came to Northwestern, our fourth stop, and people come and say, "What are you doing? Are you just taking a vacation? What kind of a thing are you?" I guess you might say we're pilgrims, and we're on a pilgrimage.

The way people always speak about truth is, "Is truth relative or absolute?" And I'd like to talk about absolute truth, and people say, "Well, how do you know anything?"

The questions about the possibility of knowing truth depend on the type of communication model of the human mind, one being like there's a fence and you throw notes over it wrapped around bricks.

Orthodox philosophy and orthodox psychology are both built on the idea that communication is just heaving the brick back and forth, and that that is the height of communication. You can do that subtler, but you can't do that any deeper. That is a materialistic idea, because in fact the most important part of us is not the meat part but the field of electrical energies which is what they call the soul, which surrounds the body, and you can see it sometimes. How many people here have seen auras at all? That's quite a few folks that have been into that particular thing.

Now I discovered that people a long time ago—thousands of years ago—were just as smart as people today, and that the finest minds of all antiquity put themselves into religion. The oldest records that we have and the ones that have been preserved with the greatest amount of respect for the longest time are religious records. The thing is, there being electricity and freeways and double-decker trains and all that kind of thing does not change the nature of people ... or change the nature of humanity's relationship to the universe.

It's just the same as when we lived in caves and gathered berries. The outer trimmings don't make us any different. What I'm saying now is the same thing as what any teacher has said in any materialistic time, which is this: If the culture teaches people to be materialistic, the culture will then find itself in the position of supplying everyone with materialistic needs and wants, and people's materialistic needs and wants cannot be satisfied.

The only kind that can be satisfied is spiritual. If you turn people on to Spirit they can live together cheaply and economically for the common good so that everyone may have their chance at Spirit, but if they're grouped together on a material sort system then they'll fight over the dwindling supply. That's what I'm coming out to say, is that we must be spiritual ... that that's the only thing that is going to help humankind over this weird little atomic–chemical hump that we've got ourselves into.

*Q: How are you going to practice Spirit in this world of chaos?*

The way we are ... the way we are. When we were in San Francisco we started doing this five years ago, and first off people said we couldn't do it at all. "Well you're just doing that in San Francisco because it's the reservation, man, it's the beatnik preserve ... that's the only reason you can do it."

So we took off on the road with two hundred of San Francisco's finest, and we've been out across Oregon and Idaho and Montana and Yellowstone Park and North Dakota and Minnesota and we've had beautiful cooperation from everybody down the road, who have been allowing us to live this kind of life because of the way we be. An Iowa Highway Patrol officer said ... we had a long conversation in which he said, "Let it be." And he said, "Rest easy." But the finest thing I thought he said was, "You don't look scary to me and I don't want to be scary to you, and maybe we can work it out." And I thought that that was a nice thing for him to tell me, because it wasn't even subtle or anything, it was right out in the open, flat out, and really neat, straight communication. We've had a lot of that, because we're being peaceful, not just advocating or saying peace.

*Q: What do you mean by* karma?

Karma can sometimes be partially expressed as taking a full swing at a golf ball in a tile bathroom. You know, it's going to get you. Here are some of the ways karma moves on a practical level: Karma can sometimes be described as subconscious physical uptightness—like a muscle that you've kept tight for so long that you've forgotten it's that way. People have great complexes of that kind of thing. In fact that kind of stuff determines how you look. The expressions on your face are almost more important for how you look than the meat part. People can just change radically by changing that kind of stuff, and that's subconscious to them, and you can think of karma as stored subconscious on that level ... a psychological-physical, psyche-soma level.

[Q: unintelligible] This is the question of reincarnation, and I don't believe in reincarnation. I also think that reincarnation is like Buddhist "Original Sin."

Buddha taught that there is no support for the soul doctrine of reincarnation. The model structure that I like about that is that some of our karma is our nature for being material. We accept certain karma for being in the material plane at all—we accept material-plane karma. That means that if you step off the edge ... *whee-e-e* ... all that.

The karma we work out is not our personal karma but our collective karma. There's a Sufi story of the river coming down to the edge of the sand and can't get across the desert, and the wind comes along and says, "Drop your identity as water and become air with me and I'll take you across the desert and turn you into water and drop you back down on the other side." And the river says, "How will I know I'll be the same river?" It doesn't matter—river is river, life is life, karma is karma. We all do our stuff. Karma's the name of the way we do it.

[Q: unintelligible] That's a conceptual, intellectual understanding. Understand sometimes means, Yes, I read that signal and can translate it and rephrase it, and sometimes understand means stand under. You can understand it the first way without understanding it the other way.

Q: [unintelligible] Sure, soul can evolve. The whole soul of life evolves. We all evolve together. We live to grow. We're part of a life cycle. Like there are some kinds of creatures that live in the water and lay their eggs on the land. Well, we're creatures that live in the Spirit world and lay our eggs in the material plane.

*Q: When you pull a chunk of bad karma out of the system, where does it go? How do you neutralize it?*

If, when people be unkind to you, you say, "Well they don't know what they're doing, they're only doing that because they're uptight and I'll just repair myself and not complain," you can take a piece of unkindness out of the universe. But if someone puts a piece of unkindness onto you and you say, "Well I'm not going to keep this," and you put it onto the next person you come to, then it starts multiplying, and that's karma.

You can make your universe better or worse by how you respond to it. Anybody who wants to can bring anybody down to a degree, you know, just by messing with their electricity physically, knock them off their energy, knock them down or hassle them for so long ... that kind of thing. If you just go ahead and accept something like that and don't try to put it back on the other fellow, don't try to make him take it, when you work it out by yourself, then you're taking it out of the universe and dissipating it. And when you relax, you release the energy that is tied up there and allow it to go free back into the universe so someone else can manifest pure, good, and healthy with it. It's the same universe; that life force is the same stuff, homogenous through the universe. Everybody partakes of a common pool.

*Q: Is there a right agreement?*

It's not a question of right agreement or wrong agreement, it's a question of agreement or no agreement, and you can tell what the agreement is because that's what all this is. This is what we agreed on, because here we are. Now my function as a teacher is to try to tell us that this is the agreement—this is how good the agreement is now—and if we want to have it better here and in the world, then we have to make our agreement better.

I think we could arrange this room a little more efficiently by moving around and stuff, so let's take a break and let me go over and check on our child that's being born.

INA MAY GASKIN: *When the first woman on the Caravan went into labor, our buses and trucks were all huddled together in a lot on the Northwestern campus. The sun was was about to set, and Stephen was getting ready to go to the auditorium for his talk.*

*There was a knock on our bus door. The pregnant woman's partner came to ask if Stephen would come and help with the birth. Because we had no midwife, doctor, or nurse among us, I suppose he thought that Stephen's combat experience in Korea might have prepared him in some way for helping at a birth.*

*At any rate, seeing that Stephen was being pulled in two directions and because I secretly wanted to be a midwife someday anyway, I quickly volunteered to go. I had never witnessed any creature being born, let alone a human, and I had never even seen a drawing or a photo of birth. However, I had talked to several women who had given birth at home, and all were sure that they had made the right choice. Since my only experience having a baby had been in a hospital and I had been forced into having anesthesia and a forceps delivery that I neither wanted nor needed, I understood why this woman had no intention of going to a hospital for this, her third, birth.*

*Going to help her was one of the best decisions I ever made in my life. It was a real fork in the road for me, and I have never regretted the fork I chose.*

*I can't imagine a better birth to have witnessed as my first. To my surprise (I had thought a laboring woman would probably look scared and bedraggled), she was radiant and incredibly beautiful as she labored, and I was entranced. I kept eye contact with her and helped her keep a slow pace of deep breathing. I think this helped her and me keep from being scared. The deep breathing seemed to be sufficient to deal with any pain or fear she was experiencing. She kept saying, between contractions, "Please stay with me," which was what I wanted to do anyway.*

*The energy that I felt in that little school bus with its clear plastic dome skylight reminded me of how my labor had felt before I was given the anesthesia. Colors were intensified, and it seemed as if I was seeing the world with new eyes.*

*It wasn't long before the laboring mother began to push. Within a few minutes, her baby boy was born. He breathed and cried without any assistance. His father tied off his umbilical cord with a shoelace that had been sterilized in a pot of boiling water on the stove. The entire process, including the expulsion of the placenta and the baby's first try at breast-feeding, proceeded so smoothly that it would have been impossible for anyone to have witnessed such a birth and not be impressed, touched, and instructed by it.*

*[Stephen returns after the break.]* The baby was born. It's a boy. We waited out the watch. Thank you very much for helping with the baby.

This is such a nice size room for conversation I think that's what we ought to keep doing … just the right size so everybody can hear what's going on. Ask your questions for everybody and so everybody can hear them.

*[Q: unintelligible]* People perceive through one way or another, either being just telepathic on the natch, or through drugs, or through having a religion that works for you and gets you high so you can see things … whatever works well.

People have always been able to see something besides this happening. Now that thing that they talk about as the land where there's ghosts or the hereafter or the beyond or something like that is the continuum that goes from thing to no-thing, or Spirit. There's a continuum that goes through there. One model structure they talk about is Earth, Heaven, and Hell, because you can generally see or be aware of a plane on either side of the one you're on. There's a continuing succession of planes, some more hellish than others, some more heavenly than others, but from any given point in that continuum you can see the closest to you.

*Q: How do you relate to time?*

I use clocks and calendars so I can get to appointments on time—get to Northwestern on the right day and that kind of thing—but as far as time goes, I don't allow myself to be fooled into thinking that 1970 is any more special than any other year or any other time, or that the condition that we find ourselves in now is any more modern or any more progressive than any place where we've been in any other time. The United States is just like the Middle Ages or the early ages or any other place. Just because we have a lot of ninety-degree angles and electricity doesn't make us much different. In that matter I don't see time at all. It's just us monkeys working it out, and it's always heavy when us monkeys are working it out. That's our trip and we just do it.

*Q: What reason do you have to think that there is any plane other than the physical plane?*

Observation. To me it feels like perfection is the best focus you can get on it, is all there is, but that as your focuses are off, surrounding planes surround it as diffraction–diffusions of reality—and you can either trip around out there in the diffractions and things or you can come right on to the Diamond Jewel in the Lotus—reality straight on as it comes.

Reality as it comes is understanding that karma is instantaneous in the here and now all the time. You create your universe by how you be through the medium of cause and effect, which is karma, and that medium is instantaneous. It's not like you do something and then some years later something happens to you. It's like if you hit, you're striking yourself—it's all one in the here and now. And if you realize that, then you're in control of your universe, which is to say that you realize that you're creating your universe. When you realize that you're creating your universe, then where are you? What are you doing?

*[Q: unintelligible]*    Linear means in a line ... has to do with space, because the idea of a line is a space thing. You've got to have space to have a line. That's how you can determine what space is—by lines and planes and solids and stuff.

The astral plane doesn't have anything out of it to use for measuring sticks, it hasn't got any time for you to tell how long it took you to get from here to there in. It just doesn't work on those rules. Non-space/time rules are nonetheless just as real, no more illusion or less illusion than the space/time kind, and in fact most of the heavy decisions are made in the non-space/time one. See, the material plane proceeds from the spiritual plane, not the other way around.

[Q: unintelligible]   Physical ego and soul and Spirit? Spirit is one with the universe, and everybody's spirit is one. Like they have the oil wells and they have separate holes that all drill into the same pool, so Spirit is the same pool that we all are. Soul is like our oil well shaft, and the body is like the derrick. It's all a continuum—it's how we connect with the universe. We are apparently separate on the physical plane, but the higher up you get you realize the less difference it makes, and it gets to the point where you see that it makes no difference whatsoever, that we're all really one.

[Q: unintelligible]   Your personality is your junk heap—that's all the spare parts you picked up along the way. Your soul is your electrical field, which is generated by your body–mind complex. Or your soul can be so out of communication with your consciousness that it doesn't know about you and you don't know about it, which is the technical description of a "lost soul."

The Spirit is non-space/time and can't have any personality or ego or anything like that. The soul is the electrical field that's created by the interaction within yourself of yourself and everybody else in the universe, and it's a direct result of this life. Like Gandhi ... his title was Mahatma, remember? Well, *maha* is great and *atma* is soul. That's like describing Gandhi's soul, which was so great that thousands and thousands of people could inhabit it at once, and the way that they got India free from England was because there was something in India that could be one thing any time the Mahatma would spark it. He could go into a random crowd and his soul was so great that he could make it be one thing.

[Q: unintelligible]   Being uptight or angry or things like that causes you to become disconnected from your soul, the electrical field surrounding your body being a result of your emotions, thoughts ... your electro-chemical trip. If you make your material self pure, you purify and extend your soul. Now the *Tibetan Book of the Dead* and the *Egyptian Book of the Dead* and the principles in the Catholic Church for the shriving of the dead man, or Extreme Unction for a man who is dying, are all precautionary measures that people may die in a sane, meditative state in order that they don't mess up their electrical field too bad.

[*Q: unintelligible*]    If you've led a bad life you might not die well, because it takes great strength of character for you to die well. You see, I belong to the sudden school, and I believe that once you realize the unsulliable nature of the intellect that it's no longer necessary to seek absolution for past sins, and that doctrine is so potent that anyone who hears it and understands it has their past sins absolved.

This idea of the unsulliable nature of the intellect is from the Tibetan tradition as reported by Y.W. Evans-Wentz in *Tibetan Yoga and Secret Doctrines.* I once was smoking some very smart grass, and I began to think about the unsulliable nature of the intellect, and I thought, This is like the difference between hardware crazy and software crazy. If you are hardware crazy, you need to learn to work around it or seek medical help. If you are software crazy, the unsulliable nature of the intellect comes into play.

A computer has two kinds of memory. One kind is called ROM or read-only memory. This means that it is a permanent, unchangeable set of instructions that tells the computer how to do normal operations like work the mouse or make type on the screen.

The other kind is called RAM, which stands for random-access memory. This is the actual working memory of the computer. It can take any form—such as a game or a check register or a word processor—that the software dictates.

New computer users are told there is nothing you can say to a computer by the keyboard that will break it or ruin it. If you manage to confuse it enough with conflicting instructions, the most that can happen is it might lock up. In that case, you just restart it and all those mistakes are erased and the RAM comes back clean and perfect. This is the unsulliable nature of the random-access memory.

You can't break or ruin the mind by anything you think. Your mind must be able to think anything. It must be able to consider all alternatives no matter how awful or horrible. Your intellect is a perfect computer. If your mind couldn't consider all the alternatives, that would be something wrong in itself. It does not make you crazy to think a crazy thought. You can look at that crazy thought and say to yourself, "My, what a crazy thought," and go on about your life without having any fear that your mind has been damaged or dirtied in any lasting way by that passing nutty thought. This is the unsulliable nature of the intellect.

*Q: Is there an essence of what is right and what is wrong?*

The moral code is simple and obvious and everybody really knows what it is and the children know what it is. Kids can go along and they can argue about how many balls you're supposed to use in three-cornered catch or anything like that, but there's always a place where all the kids will agree and will say, "Hey, that ain't fair," and they'll all agree on that.

And everybody knows what's fair, everybody knows what's just, it's really simple. It's been put down in words for thousands of years—the Sermon on the Mount, the Ten Commandments—it says, "Thou shalt not steal." I was reading a local quote–hip–unquote newspaper which was talking about how it was cool to rip off, how so long as it's only General Motors you can go ahead and steal from them because it doesn't matter. It may not matter to General Motors— General Motors may be able to write it off on taxes, and it may not matter to them a bit—but it matters terribly to your soul to do the action, never mind who you do it to.

*Q: ... So when man comes into the world, an unborn baby, already in essence he will know what is right and what is wrong?*

I believe that when a baby comes into the world that he's perfectly telepathic and a perfect Buddha and in better command of the situation than anybody around, and that he's only taught to fall from perfection by his parents' bad habits, and that if parents didn't give their children any bad habits they'd stay perfect, and that you can get back to purity, and the way to it is to discover what is the unconditioned monkey. The footsteps of the Buddha and of the unconditioned monkey are the same.

*Q: What is spiritual enlightenment?*

The first hallmark is being compassionate. I've seen all kinds of psychedelic displays, of folks that could show me colors and things, and folks that were very telepathic and could make lots of stuff happen around them, visually and like that, and some of them have not been cool. The only thing I recognize as being cool is being compassionate and doing your best to help out.

*Q: Help what out?*

I don't know what you want to call it. I want to call it life and think it's beautiful, and I feel that I am life and so I help life.

*Q: Where is the center of the universe?*

I feel that this life is the ultimate as we know it. Right here and now is the ultimate as we know it. If it isn't heavy for you, then you're not tuned in, because it's very heavy here and now, and somewhere else isn't where it's heavy. This is the center of the universe, you know, and the next time anybody else asks that question somewhere down the road, then that's the center of the universe, but this is, too.

I'd like to stay all night, but can't do it ....

Peyote is another kind of trip. Peyote's like the family problem solver; it's psychedelic-powered group therapy with a set of thousand-year-old ground rules called the peyote ritual. The peyote ritual is an interesting thing to study, because it's how a culture that had no ban against psychedelics built a psychedelic ritual over a period of thousands of years on a natural trial-and-error evolutionary basis, and you can look and see how it worked.

Now the peyote ritual has things that seem immediately barbaric perhaps … like there's a rattle, there's a staff, and you got a fan with feathers. And the staff signifies the same thing the staff always signifies, it signifies kingship or the scepter. When you're holding the staff it means that you're the chief.

Well, the staff rotates from person to person around the meeting, and with the staff goes a rattle. The rattle is a rhythm-keeping device. Next to the staff and the rattle comes the drum. Now the purpose of the drum is that, as each man is holding the staff and the rattle, he then sings his song … each man in a meeting is supposed to sing a song. Well, singing a song is saying his piece. You're supposed to make up your song extemporaneously on the spot, and I've heard men make up songs like … singing, "Get it on for Jesus, get it on for Jesus, and if you can't get it on for Jesus get it on for me, 'cause the peyote's makin' me sick. Get it on for Jesus, get it on for Jesus …." That was his song. And so the man with the staff and the fan and the rattle is singing his song, saying what he has to say to the meeting.

Well, maybe he's saying, "That cat across the room from me is witchin' me, that dude across the room ain't straight, he's bringing bad vibes in the meeting…." Maybe that's the song.

Or maybe the song is, "I see and understand the relationship of the universe to humankind at this time, and I want to communicate that to y'all...." That might be a song. The thing with the drum is that nobody has to sing his song without at least one person who has to pay attention to his riff and help him out.

So nobody speaks alone; everybody's got at least one man paying attention and covering for him, helping him out. And that man has got to pay at least good enough attention to drum for him, because the man with the rattle sets the drumming pace, and the man with the drum is supposed to follow and keep him amplified and keep him going.

So each person has a chance, with somebody to help him out, to say his thing. And that's how that ritual was evolved. Other things in the ritual are like you're not supposed to walk between certain people at certain times during the ceremony. Well, that means that you aren't supposed to walk between somebody and the road chief while the road chief is looking in his eyes or anything, because it's a telepathic communication, and you'd interrupt it. The rest of the rules are mostly about how people shouldn't blow each other's energy, how to let the vibes really grow high and stay high.

So, very good feelings around peyote, because of its purity. Nothing ambiguous about it in that sense. It's a cactus. They say that with peyote that the heavier the road chiefs get, the less peyote they need to eat. Now, peyote sometimes means the cactus, and sometimes it means that you have to do a little penance. Sometimes a road chief has been heard to say to someone who's complaining, "Shut up and eat your peyote."

The last healing I was in on was myself this morning. I had a flu thing that had been going through our family, and it was my turn and I was having it a couple of days. It was the kind that puts you in chills and fever, and ache. If I'd move my eyes, the muscles of my eyeballs hurt. It just did that for a couple of days, and I was hassling it.

And then this morning Ina May decided that although I was a pretty sad and sickly-looking thing and not at all a turn-on, that she was going to try to turn me on, and get me off … if she could … like raising Lazarus or something, I was so pale and puny. And she did. And she put energy into me until I started realizing that if I could just get off that I'd be cool, because I didn't have enough energy to even be interested in sex … and I wasn't interested in sex at all. And then somewhere I got where, well, I was a little interested … And then I got to where I thought, I can make it, man, with help … And then I did. Well, it wasn't bang-bang flash-flash-flash, like usual, it was one bang, and then the rest of it was just my body going s-s-s-s … and filling back up again, because I was just drained dry. And I just filled up off of that energy—that sexual energy. Between us we generated sexual energy, and then she let me have it, she let me have the juice.

And I stood up out of bed and I looked down at my bod, and the day before I'd looked like a skinny old man, and I looked down and I didn't look like a skinny old man, I looked good to me. I said, "Far out, I feel good" … and stretched a little bit, danced a little … everything's fine … And it was just right there, that's non-conceptual healing—applying life energy to heal an ailment. I still got traces of it, but I'm on my feet and rolling and feeling good … you know, over the top.…

What we're really here for tonight is communion. That means when a bunch of monkeys come together and they're going to be together and relax and let their things all hang out. It's okay if we be quiet for a while now and then. It lets us get smarter, so the next thing will be a better thing anyway.

The first time I ever found out about energy was with the use of psychedelics. Here and now I don't think everybody is stoned on psychedelics, but it seems to be very stoned. The way we be stonedest best together is if we each one take responsibility for our own share of the vibration.

What I'm doing now is like housework for our group head—getting this head integrated so it'll be like all one head and then it'll be a smart head. One of the heaviest things going is about the nature of attention. Attention is energy—just an equal sign in there—attention is energy. So when you pay attention to me here and now, you're giving me juice—giving me energy—and with that energy I'm supposed to do what I can with it in some way to make it come back to you in a way that's a learning thing for all of us.

A lot of us went to San Francisco in response to a dream ... that we had heard, "Wow, man, they're getting into Spirit and stuff out there."

I'd been teaching at San Francisco State College. I'd gotten my Bachelor's degree there, I'd gotten my Master's degree there, and then I was teaching there, because I didn't know what else to do.

That was just about at the time that the Haight-Ashbury was beginning to happen in San Francisco, which I at the time didn't know about, but I noticed that a bunch of my students were leaving school. I wondered what they were finding better, so I started hanging out with some of my students.

I fell in with folks that took dope, because that's what was happening in Haight-Ashbury. And I remember when the Haight-Ashbury was as pure and clean ... you know, it was like a flower, a newborn baby or something, because everybody walking around the streets was bright-eyed, stoned, and on a good trip, and understanding what a good trip was, and putting out some work and some energy to create a good trip—a massive good trip—so good that lots of people would like it. And that's what it started out to be, and somewhere along the line it got into like ... I remember when Haight Street was pure, before it got hit by methedrine, politics, and heroin. During that time I was taking psychedelics, and I learned about whole new planes of experience that I'd never known the existence of before, that were just as valid as the ones I had known before. Isn't that what happens when you come on stoned and see that whole other level?

When they say that man does not live by bread alone, they mean that we're kind of vibratory amphibians, and part of our amphibious body lives here in this medium, but part of us is electrical and vibratory, and that's a whole world there, and we live in that world, too. I don't know hardly what to call that world. Carl Gustav Jung called it the collective unconscious. The yogis in India called it the astral plane. To me it seems to be a continuum of vibrational planes that continue in degrees of subtlety and purity until you reach one of absolute purity, of spiritual purity, and between the material plane and the plane of absolute spiritual purity this continuum exists where the illusion gets thicker as you come down away from Spirit. This is fairly thick illusion here. [*Knocks on platform.*] There's some just a little thinner than that. It's not quite thick enough that you can bang on it, but if you're stoned enough you can see it, and it goes on out to where maybe you can't see it so much but you can feel it with other perceptors.

So the first thing that happened when I got stoned was I didn't just turn on …. Well I did in a lot of ways, because there's that fantastic place where you get stoned, where you say, "Oh yeah? Really? Far out!" And you find out that it's really cool after all, that the universe is cool. And that happened. But a bunch of other things happened too, because taking psychedelics makes you telepathic.

Think about the implications of that. What if you be telepathic around people who have funny stuff in their heads? What if you be telepathic around thousands of people at a time who have funny stuff in their heads? That means that your telepathic perceptors can be bombarded with such an input that you can't integrate it.

Now that happened to the whole Haight Street culture at a point, and that was the beginning of what they call psychedelic art. Psychedelic art is a picture of somebody's trip when they weren't able to integrate what they saw. Anybody understand that? Like the first kind of stuff I saw while tripping was all kinds of things—forms, shapes, colors—happening. Then it got so I didn't see that kind of stuff so much. I just started seeing what was really there in front of me, real good, better than I had ever seen it, so I understood everything that was happening in it.

And I realized that all the information I ever needed was right in front of my eyes all the time. Psychedelic vision at that level—all the little squirls and squigglies and fancies and colors and all that—becomes meaningful information that you can integrate and take information out of and navigate by, just the same as you do ordinary vision.

Well, now I get into the thing of ordinary vision and psychedelic vision. There isn't any such thing as ordinary vision and psychedelic vision; it's psychedelic and more psychedelic, because vision at all is psychedelic vision. Having eyes to look out there lets your consciousness out farther. Having ears extends your consciousness out farther. Learning something new extends your consciousness out farther. Learning of the existence of another town over the hill that you didn't know about extends your consciousness out farther, expands your mind, expands your consciousness. So everybody all of a sudden learned of whole new planes of existence and got their consciousness expanded. Blew a bunch of minds, including mine. I was really nutty for a while. I'd go around, I'd try to put on people what I was seeing, and they'd say, "You're crazy, man." I'd say, "All right." But the next trip I'd look and there it would be again.

I started taking psychedelics so far back that it was legal and considered to be a random experience, that you didn't know what was going to happen, just a random old thing. And then I started seeing the same kind of thing happen over and over again. I started seeing that there was some stuff in there that wasn't random at all; it was very orderly ... that if you said something that was a downer it ran the juice out, that if you told a lie you'd drop your energy, if you were mean to someone you'd drop your energy, if you went on an ego trip you'd drop your energy ... it would get weird. If someone who was on the trip with you wasn't being straight with you, it would get the trip weird for everybody.

Now I want to talk about one of the stable data of my entire philosophical trip, which is the phenomenon of the contact high. And the reason I think that's important to talk about is that my experience of the contact high just happened by sweet luck to be a perfect experiment, and showed me something that I did not know before.

I hadn't smoked hardly any dope ever in my life, and a friend of mine gave me a joint. I had it in my wallet for a while. And we were staying down below San Francisco, down in Daly City in a very nice house on the edge of a golf course, which belonged to a woman in my creative writing class who said she wanted to sponsor me and my wife and baby to be down there in that nice house and use her car to go to school and help get me through my graduate school, which was very sweet of her.

And this lady Ollie and my wife were inside talking to one another, chatting, and I stepped out onto the driveway and found that old joint in my wallet, and I smoked it. And I went back in and sat around for a while, and I noticed that they were talking over there, and I went over and joined their conversation.

We talked a little while, and I felt that I was actually pretty stoned off that joint. And then in a little bit, I began to notice that so were they; they were getting a contact high off of me, and they didn't smoke dope, and they didn't know I smoked dope, and they didn't know I had dope in me right now ... and it was a perfect experiment—without any knowledge in any way, the contact high was shown in clear relief. And if you can get one signal across—the signal of being stoned—other signals can pass.

Well, if you stop and think about that for a minute, it's an outrageous thing. What it means is the message of stonedness is sent telepathically. Right? You can send any kind of message including stonedness as a telepathic message. That's how you can get a contact high.

[Q: unintelligible]   I think white light is your nervous system letting go ... flash ... I had that happen. It just blew out everything I had. Now that's the first kind of overamp; that's your whole nervous system —bang, white light, white sound, white taste, white bod, everything.

By white sound I mean the radio concept of when the signal coming through blankets the entire frequency so no signal may be discerned then. Well, with psychedelics that's when the psychic world— the telepathic world—is coming in on you so strong that it's blowing you completely out—no message, just input.

Then you get to where you see pretty colorful curls and squigglies ... which means you can integrate it out of white light into something anyway, and then you can bring it from there to looking just like ordinary, except very high.

The highest place I am, usually, is very clear, it isn't a bit funny looking. It's very clear and very pretty. Very good vision and very good detail is what real good psychedelic vision is like.

So with all this stuff I'm trying to give you a broad picture of a cultural happening and what happened to me as an individual member of that culture as it came along—those people who stumbled into psychedelics like Aldous Huxley, who said you can be one with the universe that way. Aldous Huxley was the closest thing to a saint that I'd seen at that time. Aldous Huxley was a pure man, and his mind was so fine that I just believed what he said. So when I took psychedelics, I took them on his recommendation.

But I don't take initials anymore. I quit taking initials. Just organic stuff that grows in the ground. I don't like initials because I want to know whose initials.

Well, I split the city and I went away for seven or eight months, traveled around, went down to British Honduras and hung out under the Crown grape trees and smoked grass, tried to get my head together.

I got back to the city quite a while later, not knowing much, knowing there was something heavy to be known, but not knowing what it might be, and I continued on doing the psychedelic thing for a while. I had one perfect trip, where I saw how it worked. I got to shinny all the way up the flagpole and hang on to the top of the flagpole long enough to get a good look. You know, found out how the universe works.

Now that's an outrageous thing, but I'm prepared to sit here and tell you how the universe works, and I can impart that knowledge to you:

*As you sow, so you shall reap.*

So when I understood that, I realized that on one level that wasn't a very big thing to understand. They always tell us that. But what I found out on that trip was that it was true … here and now, all the time. And I thought, Well, if that was such an outrageous surprise to me, it may be interesting to other folks. Of course, all my thinking at the time wasn't all this logical and all in a row as it is when I'm telling you now. I was still kind of fumbling around, a little mind-blown. It's hard to keep track of things when the whole universe turns on.

Well, when I went to try to communicate that thing to some people at the Experimental College at San Francisco State, I didn't know exactly what I was doing except I wanted to communicate that thing. So we set up Monday Night Class. Actually I didn't set up Monday Night Class. Experimental College had an empty hole on Monday night. That's a safe one. We know that's cool because it just fell down that way.

The way you know things are cool is you name them by the right names. Later on we started having Sunday morning service, which we called by the name of Sunday Morning Service.

So I started interacting with the beatnik community of San Francisco, and I began to realize that I was serving the function of a parish priest because I was taking care of the spiritual needs of a little community. I just learned how to do that on some kind of on-the-job training thing, and it scared me about the first time I found out I was doing it. I asked for advice from Suzuki Roshi on that, and the only advice I could get was, "Go carry your own mail, I got my own route." So I went back and kept doing it. I copped at that time to being a teacher and do now.

Does that bring us up close to here and now? Are we caught up to date? Okay then, the main thing I have to say is that none of us are going to get high until all of us get high and all of us can't get high while some of us are bringing some of us down. And it doesn't matter who you bring down, it brings the whole universe down. If you bring a cop down, it brings the whole universe down. When I made that kind of realization, I began to notice that I could no longer tell the difference between cops and kids, cowboys and Indians, none of that. All *Homo sapiens*—monkeys here on the rock, and if the monkeys on the rock don't make it, the universe has no attachment. Which means we better shape up, man. That's mainly what I have to say.

Then behind that there is something about enlightenment. Well I can't tell you enlightenment—it can't be communicated verbally, and it may not be discerned by Aristotelian two-valued logic. It's much like being a grownup and knowing where it's at and being smart ... being on top of your thing.

So that being like a little spread of subject matter of what we're prepared to talk about—life, death, love, religion, dope, politics, or anything else that anyone wants to bring up—I'd like to turn to a question and answer thing now, because what this really is for me is a dialogue.

*[Q: unintelligible]*   We've driven across the United States from San Francisco with fifty buses to help me say what I can say. And I'm willing to keep saying it as long as anybody will help me say it. That's some of what I'm doing here in Ann Arbor is asking for your help too, to say this thing: that it ain't cool to kill people, that we got to be together, all of us together on this planet, that we can't waste any of us ... and I'm saying that. It's really important that that be said, and I'm saying that louder than anybody else is saying that right now.

I'm somebody who was born in this country, had this country's kind of a religious upbringing, which is sort of half-assed. Now when I say religion, I mean any religion that says that all of us are necessary.

I can't cop to a religion or a political system that says everything is cool as soon as we croak these folks here. I can't buy any of that.

I don't know anybody who if they really think about it wants to hurt a cop, because that isn't relevant. What you want is the cop to do his job, take care of traffic, help little ladies across the street, keep the burglars from busting into the grocery store, that trip.

There's nothing served by hurting them, so how about if you can just talk the cop into being groovy. We've been coming out across the country in no way camouflaged. We take up ten or twenty miles of highway when we're rolling. When we come through a town the people's vibes stay good and they keep smiling and their eyes are shiny, but their hands begin to drag after a while because they get tired of waving to so many of us.

We have been in massive engagements with the police of eight or ten states across the country, and I have not sold out anything I believe in to deal with any of those cops. All I have done is treat them as human beings—as I would like to be treated—tell them what we were doing, and the way has been made open for us. We have been treated well, shown where to park, not hassled, taken good care of.

*[Q: unintelligible]* I teach nonviolence, but I also teach, "Don't go in the army." You can ask me questions about how not to, but I think everybody already knows any way they want to, as long as you don't screw your soul up too bad by lying. It seems to me that nobody has to lie about not going in the army, and it seems if you have nerve enough to tell the real truth that you don't have to go, which is, "I do not agree with killing as a means of settling human differences and will not participate in any form of it to any extent."

*Q: You'll go to jail.*

I'd rather spend two years in jail than two years in the army. Much rather. And I'd rather spend my life in jail than kill somebody.

When we OM this time, everybody come on as strong as you can. This is a real good-sounding room, really good acoustics in here, so if we come on strong we ought to really get it off.

That's really nice when we all stop together spontaneously, you know, everybody paying attention to the same thing and knowing what's happening. That's really good there. Let's go on with questions.

*[Q: unintelligible]* There's philosophical discussions of free will that say there's free will and determinism, and they make a dichotomy out of it, and it's either one or the other. But free will is on a continuum, and the most determined you can be is to be totally subconscious. Stuff that's in your subconscious is stuff that you don't know about that's changing you—stuff that you're being determined by. The less subconscious you have, the more free will you have, as you go along. Well, everybody has free will at one point at least, which is, Are you going to straighten up or not?

*[Q: unintelligible]*   Death works like this: We're all born and we all die. Credit and debit—the books balance. No need to fear it. Relax, it will happen when it's going to happen. There is no need to fear the sudden fear. That's out of Proverbs in the Bible. There is no need to fear the sudden fear. If it's been cool so far, it will be cool, so straighten up.

*[Q: unintelligible]*   Oh yeah, I'm in love with hundreds and hundreds of people. I'm just completely in love with hundreds and hundreds of people at a time, and I'm always gassed when one of my lady friends gets married.

*Q: I understand that celibacy is one of the paths, but I have a feeling that family life is the harder path.*

Right. I'm a householder yogi. A householder yogi is the hard kind. It's a cop-out to go to a celibate monastery. Life is a puzzle and a riddle, and if you go to that kind of monastery that means, I give up. The really heavy thing is to try to stay stoned and do good and all that right there in the middle of it … right in with the family, make decisions like what are you going to do about your kids, and what do you do about your old lady. The way of the householder yogi is a hard goer.

I also teach tantric yoga … that you can get high making love. Tantric yoga can also be thought of as the fine art of turning the lead in your pants into lead in your pencil. And you're supposed to be high making love. You can get telepathic and psychedelic making love. The way you do it is to keep at it long enough to build up some juice instead of blowing it for the flash in a couple of minutes.

I think we've come to a good agreement. We ought to quit before we're tired instead of waiting till we're tired. This has been really fine for me here. I've really enjoyed this one a lot. What I enjoyed is that you asked the kind of questions that let me say the kind of things that I really wanted to say. It's really been good that way with you.

God Bless you, Ann Arbor, and all that. See you another time.

The first time that I smoked grass I was seventeen and I smoked it with a fellow who kind of played with my mind for a while. He took me out to the edge of a curb, and he said, "Look down there at the edge of that canyon. See the rocks and the rapids? See the white water breaking around the rapids?"

And he pushed me off. I landed a few inches down, stiff-kneed with a jolt, thinking that I really was going off a cliff. So I didn't smoke any more grass for ten years, and on my twenty-seventh birthday this dude came into my study where I was writing and stuck this pipe in my mouth—a carved meerschaum pipe with a little lid on it like a German windproof pipe—and said, "Smoke this stuff."

And it was real honest-to-God Acapulco Gold, and I took several giant tokes on it, and I got kind of telepathic. And I'd look at this dude I was turning on with, and in the back of my mind I'd think, I feel like I know what's in his mind. I wonder if that's really just an illusion from this kind of dope? And his eyes would sparkle back at me and I'd think, Wow, looks like he really knows. And it got all golden and I felt good. It was my birthday party and I felt stoned on Acapulco Gold and everybody was being good to me and giving me presents. And I woke up in the morning and said, "I'm going to do a lot of that."

Since then my mind blows on childbirth, the sunlight through trees … I blew my mind on the diesel of an electric switch engine in San Francisco one time. I was sitting in the bus, and there was this switch engine outside. The way a diesel-electric works is it's got a huge diesel engine, and it turns the generator, and the generator weighs maybe two thousand pounds, and it starts revving up behind this big diesel. Well, I plugged in on the generator revving up like that and rode up with it. And it got up and it peaked out, and I kind of parachuted a little bit and thought, Far out, next time it comes by I'm going to go two for one with it. So the generator started going up and I was revving twice for what it was revving, and that got me pretty high, so I did that a couple of times—doubled up on it each time—and then I came to one where it was revving out and I realized I had finally shifted gears clear through it, because I realized that I was going to peak out before it did, and it just put me right out—stoned me with a hard rush—because I'd managed to multiply that until I couldn't integrate it anymore. My integrator blew its fuse. That's what psychedelics do—blow your ability to integrate for a while.

I also blew my mind on a bunch of masts in a yacht harbor on a stormy day. All these masts were all a different length, and they had all different keels, and they all had different kinds of waves coming around in different directions through the docks and everything, and the wind blowing, and they were just on a complete random trip. So I looked at it and I quit trying to look at anything much and kind of let my head flow free and just let that scene be like a flood scene, and then I just slammed on the integrator like I was going to understand it all at once. And I got a huge glow about eighteen inches right around my sexual chakra and it turned into juice and ran up my back and stoned me. So you can get high on just anything if you work with it a little bit.

*Q: How did you become a teacher?*

Because I felt somebody needed to do that, and I went looking for somebody to do that, and I looked for somebody to do that for years, and I couldn't find anybody doing that, and I felt somebody ought to be. It's important. And while I was looking I found that I was doing that a little bit provisionally myself, just waiting until I could find somebody who could do that, and I ended up doing it so much that I was just doing it. I take it on my own responsibility—on my own karma—anything that I say to anybody, and if I tell you something it's on the basis of my judgment, and that's the only thing I can tell it to you about, that's all I got.

*Q: Then you're saying what you think.*

Yes. It's the vision of the third eye is what it is. It means that after taking as much psychedelics and studying in spiritual things as I have, that I have some degree of psychedelic vision happening all the time. Have you ever been stoned and looked at somebody and saw into their soul? Well, I do that sometimes, to a greater or lesser degree, depending on how high I can get under the circumstances.

*Q: On the one hand people should be open to each other, and on the other hand we feel some uneasiness about people expressing anger towards each other, and I was wondering if you could see the contradiction there.*

No, it's like this: Anger closes people up. I used to know a fellow who was an anger magician, and he got his way by being angry at people. One time I watched him come on that way to a dude who was stoned on a psychedelic, and it curled the dude up like a fishworm, reduced him to tears and stomach cramps just by being angry at him. That's where anger's at.

Let's OM because it will be good for us and then go ahead and do that thing.

*Q: How do you organize your following?*

An organ grows, like an inner organ and organic and all that business. If somebody's there serving a polar function, things will organically grow around them. Suzuki Roshi came to California and sort of sat down and meditated, and they built a monastery around him because his vibrations just organized everything that happened around him. He didn't have to say, "Build that, do that, put that there." He did that, but he didn't have to. It just happened. It grew all around him.

Folks say, "Well that's a heavy thing to do. You set yourself up as a spiritual teacher, folks are going to laugh at you and things. It's going to be heavy." Well it was really heavy for the first two or three years. It isn't too hard for me anymore because I have a lot of folks helping me; I'm really taken care of well. I can't do anything anymore but just be grateful at how well I get taken care of.

But for a while I had to scratch, and whoever wants to set themselves up as a teacher, I think, can't do it with a piece of paper from the yogi school that says he's a teacher. I think he's got to interact with the community till the community finds out can he teach or is it worthwhile if he does. The organization thing … I don't believe in lists of things, column A, all that, but swap around among you, and put together a thing. That's what a Church is, isn't it?

Now what they used to use instead of psychedelics was the parish priest, and he'd say, "Ah, John, you're getting far out with beating your wife. You got to back off and stop all that, go back home and take care of your kids, don't be out here messing around all the time, straighten up, man, and get back to your family," or something like that. You ever hear anybody come on to anybody like that outside of a movie? But that needs to be done sometimes, because a lot of people are incredible wastrels and goof off all the time from being on ego trips. Now there ought to be somebody who would tell them that.

Well, here's the way the structure works out about the heavies: You get a man who can do that and who can do it pure without … he hasn't got anything to gain by it, it's not going to get him any brownie points or get him a better car or anything like that, and everybody knows that he does that all the time, and then you juice him.

Everybody who says anything, you got to talk louder. All that long hair really deadens sound.

*Q: The question I have is I was really stoned and really feeling good, living where I'm living in the dorm and dealing with the classes I'm taking, which at the present time I can't get out of because that's bad karma on my parents and other kinds of things like that. To get straight I have to deal with what I have now, and I'm really feeling fine and really up there, and interacting with other people who aren't anywhere near there is really hard, you know. I'm up there and they're not up there and I'd like to turn them on ….*

Whoa, you were running cool till right there, and then you blew it. You put in a relativity about being higher than somebody else. Nobody is higher than anybody else, we're all on the same altitude, because we all got one group head whether we cop to it or not. If you have a bunch of people sitting in a room all doing separate trips, some of them reading magazines, some of them listening to the radio, they're still a group head, that's just how they divide themselves up on the material plane. As far as the bad karma with your parents thing, you can't hang your karma on your parents, see, and like if you think that a college course ….

*Q: … Ah-ah-ah …*

Here's the way energy works: if you go "ah-ah-ah" at me while I'm in the middle of a sentence it interrupts the juice, and that's kind of an energy habit.

*Q: … Your parents' karma …*

Yeah, your parents' karma, thank you. If you feel that your college career is hanging you up spiritually, you can't say whether you quit school or not has anything to do with your parents, and if you say you can't quit school because you aren't straight with your parents, maybe what you ought to do is go get straight with your parents, then quit school. Or maybe you ought to quit school, then get straight with your parents, whichever lives closest.

*Q: How does one deal with a situation where there is no reinforcement of the high that I feel in a group?*

You can't take your reinforcement from the outside. Buddha says, "Seek no refuge outside yourself." You've got to know you're cool. The only way to know you're cool is to have been cool. So if you haven't been cool so far you better get cool, so the next time it comes up you can know you've been cool.

*Q: You make fundamental assumptions about people and you want to get straight with them. How do you get straight if they don't want to make the same assumptions?*

Here's the secret, and this is what I get a whole bunch of my juice from: Everybody's got the same fundamental assumptions. If you start at the right levels ... like I find when I say everybody's included, doesn't put anybody out, all-inclusive, excludes no one at all, I can get everybody to buy that, because everybody says, "That's good, there's room for me, far out."

The way I've been getting along with folks on the road is I start off at places like that. I don't start off with peyote tea, I start off at a place that anybody can do it, anybody can get enlightened. I don't think anybody is so screwed up they can't get enlightened. If you ever get to a place where you're so screwed up you can't get enlightened any-more, the universe notifies you. It's the same way the electric com-pany does. They cut off your switch. That's how you know you can't get enlightened in this life. But as long as you're still alive you can still get cool, and what we said about basic assumptions ... if your basic assumption is that somebody won't get cool with you, that's a shaky basic assumption. Your basic assumption should be that everybody will get cool with you if you be fair and straight with them. It may take a while.

One of the heaviest pieces of magic you can do is assume the other person's goodwill. I have looked at people when I was stoned and had them looking back at me with the cold Nazi fangs, if you know what I mean, and manifested them groovy, because I couldn't stand to look at them that way anymore.

*Q: I was rapping with a friend last night, and he's a real political heavy, and what happened was, he said he used to be where you're at. He said, "But I came back, and I know that's not where it's at in terms of helping people," and he wouldn't go any farther with me and kept giving me bad vibes if I pursued it any farther.*

Well, as far as your hassle with your friend goes, I don't know about that and can't talk about it, but I do see that I need to talk about politics a little more.

I have been comparing politics with enlightenment, which is not a very good deal, but that's not the right thing I should be thinking about. I should be thinking about politics versus armed revolution and war. Politics is much better than armed revolution and war, and I have become a political creature because I do not want to be pushed by default into a war. I also will not submit to tyranny.

So I'm working on politics, working on trying to get the Republicans to don't be such liars; I'm trying to find a good Democrat to back; I am left of any Democrat I know, but that's the only one they have a box for me that I can vote with, and I am one of the people who hopes that you will join in also at helping clean this country up and take it back from the thieves.

It's about what you mean by revolution. A revolution is supposed to set up something new, it's supposed to turn the whole thing over and put on something new.

Here's what this country is doing right now: This country was set up with guns and high ideals. Right? You can see that in your first-grade reading book with the old pilgrim with his blunderbuss ... our old images packing guns. And here we are two hundred years later, and count the high ideals and count the guns, and we got lots more guns than high ideals. That's the trouble with setting up with guns and high ideals. You got to set it up with just high ideals, and if you get wasted you start over again with just high ideals.

And you don't ever do it with guns, and you start over again with high ideals every time. The only way you can do that is you've got to be sustained by knowledge of good karma, because it's heavy to keep doing that.

I really understood what that means from going on this trip, because every way I've gone the way has been open in front of me. It's been made easy for me everywhere I've been going, and the thing is, I don't think they're making the way easy for me because I take dope and have long hair or because I'm a good orator. I think it's because I'm preaching peace. I really am preaching peace and I really am peaceful and I really teach people to be peaceful and the people around me are peaceful and you can come up to the people around me and find out that they really are peaceful, and on account of that I find that everything has been made open in front of us.

I tell you, I'd like to let us go because I've got to drive out to a highway in the morning. We've got to take our Caravan out tomorrow. We came all the way from San Francisco to talk to you and this has felt like a real conversation to me, and I feel like we really got to know each other a lot.

Okay, it's stoned, I really love you a lot and we'll see you again I'm sure some time, because we're just going to keep on doing this and I hope other folks help out, too.

God Bless you all and good night.

In traveling around I've found it's better to let everybody know what we're going to do first and then they'll be more inclined to join in. The idea is that everybody is supposed to join in. We're going to chant the OM. Some people consider it an old Hindu chant, but I consider it much older than that. I think it's the first monkey chant, because it's the simplest chant. Just open up your thing and let it all flow out. Don't be afraid that you can't or anything, just open up and pick out a good note that you can let it out on and listen to the music we make and feel how high we get, because anybody who wants to can get high right now, whether or not you ever took any psychedelics or anything like that in your life. That's not the only way you get it on. You get it on because you try to be open to one another, and you can get it on right now.

I always like to let that place after the OM hang quiet for a while because it's such a heavy perfect place.

People say, "Okay, you say you're hip to Spirit. Now what? What does that do?" Well it changes everything. It changes the whole game board of existence. It makes life an orderly process so that you can, by your actions, make what happens out there be better. You can change yourself, and through that you can change the world.

73

Here's what Spirit is: It's that thing that's the only thing heavy enough to make a monkey change his mind. Monkeys say they change their mind for patriotism and politics or love of country, but then they trade back and forth a lot, and trade sides and stuff, too. Now, Spirit being defined as the only thing heavy enough to make a monkey change his mind, it seems to me it's the only thing with a potential of making somebody think that the rest of the universe might be as important as he is.

Most people that I've met don't really think that the rest of the universe is quite as important as they are. It's them and it, and them first. That's a fairly common sort of an attitude, given this society, culture, and schooling trip. Most of the things that this college here is about, not just this one, but this one sight unseen because it's a college, because it teaches that kind of linear education—it teaches that there are things that are conceptual, one step removed from actual reality, that are more important than actual reality.

They teach in Zen Buddhism about the Diamond Jewel in the Lotus—the jewel of reality. When I come to tell you about Spirit, I come to say that reality may be apprehended, that there is an absolute truth, that the only kind of truth is not relative truth. A university is pretty much dedicated to teaching relative truth.

Also I teach, as a subheading of talking about Spirit, that you have free will, and that you can change yourself if you want to. Now most of the psychology and sociology that's taught in universities is of the brand that says everybody's so conditioned by their culture and by their society that they can't possibly do anything free anyway, and that you can't know all of the factors and so who knows and who cares, and runs it down that way, and not only says that people are determined but figures out more ways to determine people.

Now the vibrations are pretty strong in here. Here's how you can learn about what's perceivable by various people: To how many people is the vibration in here perceivable? Would you raise your hands?

Yeah, that's pretty good ... pretty good number. Now if I say there's a vibration in here perceivable, and you don't perceive it, what am I saying about the nature of our universes? That should be something of real interest to every person in this room. Now that vibration that those people raised their hands and said was perceivable to them is a function of the Spirit world. That's what we call it in English. Spirit world. In Sanskrit they call it the astral plane.

I've been trying to find out what are the English words for things like that because they've dropped out of English so much from lack of usage that they almost don't have any value in them. It's hard to find out what do they mean or do they have any juice or not because this culture has become several generations removed from Spirit in a lot of ways.

Now, not only is there that place—that world where those vibrations are, which is inter-contiguous with here and now—but what's going on there makes more difference about what happens here than what happens here does, here being assumed to be the material plane, although I'm never sure of that anymore. How's that? Is that a kind of talking that's making sense?

And this falls out of an orderly set of laws. Here's how it is: If you try to move the material plane from the material plane, it's just moving the furniture around. But if you learn how to move from the spiritual plane, you can make changes in the material plane that stay changed. Making changes in the material plane that stay changed is how you can create growth, and you can't make anything heavy except what you grow, including yourself, your family, your culture.

I feel like this would be a good time to start doing questions if there's any ... religious, nonviolent, believing in karma, free will. Karma's the law of cause and effect, as you sow so you shall reap ... you know, all of that. That should almost be enough grid-point coordinates to tell you where I'm at, if you're paying attention at all. We can start with questions right now and build a thing right here in this room—

an interaction which we have the use of this room to do, and which I'm good at helping coordinate. So let's start off with questions about anything, preferably spiritual, but I don't know what isn't spiritual.

*Q: What I feel from what I do is the Spirit that makes me do it. It is neither good nor bad. To me that is God. There is neither up nor down. It is heavy, but it is bearable.*

Sounds like barely. I find the benign indifference of the universe to be a complete blessing. I'm very glad to know the universe can't be rigged. No way to rig the universe, man, it's fair and square. Input, output. You do your thing, it does it back to you, just like you ordered. That's really one of the heaviest things I have to say—that you get it back like you ask for it. And I don't just say that and go back to some comfortable place. We're living on the road right now because we came out on the road to talk to folks.

We came from San Francisco up to Oregon, did a gig there, and we got such good reviews from our interaction with the Oregon heat that they put out police teletypes on us all the way across the rest of the country that said they liked us, and we got taken care of beautifully all the rest the way across the country, up to and including the police escort to this gig.

They brought us over from the farm where we were parked. And the towns that we stop in—small towns where we stop to gas up and do groceries and things—we hit their paper the next day, and it's like we get our report card on how did we do with that town.

As we were coming along through the south, we made quite an adventure at one little mom-and-pop store. We came in this little place to get some fuel, and I believe that we actually pumped all their gas, bought all their candy, all their pop, all their chips, almost cashed them out. I think they would have been in a great position to retire, since most of their stock was gone. And we pulled out with the Caravan and left them standing there with this great untidy handful of small bills and whatnot. It was a fine adventure for them, and we were amused by it, too.

The little towns along the way have liked us because we've been doing that thing I'm teaching—that you get back what you put out. Doing that has made the way open for us, has made people love us and take care of us and be good to us and be down home.

*Q: One of the things that's been happening to me is when I do Zen meditation or when I'm reading Zen texts, I feel like everything I'm doing is fine. But when I read Christian texts, like the Aquarian Gospel for instance, I get a great sense of distance between me and what Jesus was, and it gets me uptight a little bit that I've got such a long way to go, and I just … Can you resolve that at all?*

Christianity is an either-or flip-of-a-coin kind of a religion. You're either going to go to Heaven or Hell for all of eternity on one chance on the wheel. That's a very heavy trip, and because of that Christianity has an outrageous Christ-and-devil structure strung way out apart from each other. Now the thing I like about Christ is compassion and the refusal to be dragged away from the people. That's what Christ has that's really fine. Buddha has that, too. Christ was born a carpenter and stayed cool with the carpenters, you know. But Buddha was born a prince and became cool with everybody.

I don't know if people know exactly how that worked, but Buddha was born a prince and his father had decided that he should never have any evil happen to him, everything should be just rosy for him so nothing would ever turn his mind away from being the king, which was what he was raised to be, and somewhere along the line he wandered outside the temple and he saw somebody dying and he saw somebody sick and he saw somebody old and he said, "Yark, what's that!"

And they hipped him that that kind of thing went on, which he hadn't known until that time, at which time he completely blew the king thing. Went out in the woods and sat around on brown rice and meditated for many years … other things, all the religious disciplines, whatever he could. He tried every way there was to try to find a way to get off, to try to find a way to justify the way he'd been raised with what he saw outside the gates, and the only way he could justify it was to include it and become it and be it.

Now the thing they have in Christianity that's heavy is morality, and this country really needs morality. This is an immoral country, man. I know I sound like those dudes in the Old Testament, but this is an immoral country, and I don't mean just like Vietnam. That's outrageous immoral, that's criminal. But I mean the country itself is immoral.

People don't have a positive value on the idea of being honest with your fellow monkeys. Well, what makes a civilization function is that the monkeys agree to be honest with one another, and if that isn't the agreement then, man, you've got to sleep with your pistol under your head, because you don't know who'll come rip you off.

So Christianity has moral structure and that's what this country could really get from Christianity, but I just can't hack Christian psychology. Christian psychology makes a picture of the psyche that makes it too hard to handle or too scary.

But Buddhist psychology is outrageous—the cleanest, most beautiful look at the mind that I think mankind has taken. Buddhist psychology makes American psychology look like it's in kindergarten. It's amazing, and it's an ancient, ancient psychology; it's been around a long time. Western culture comes on like Freud discovered the unconscious. He didn't. It's been the working tool of every priest, road chief, shaman, medicine man, what have you, as long as we were this kind of monkeys.

I think that's one of the heaviest things that could be said at a college like this. It's to get hip to the two-valued-ness of the culture and that you've got to do what you can to get out of the two-valued-ness of the culture. If the system by which you apprehend the universe is too clumsy, it makes you get a clumsy universe back. And if you apprehend the universe more subtly, you get a more subtle universe back.

Now the thing is, anybody who's curious about any of these things I say is supposed to raise their hand at any point and say, "Hey, I don't know what you're talking about," or something like that, because if you're sitting there and you don't know what's happening, you're subconscious in this group head.

This is a group head, and a group head responds the same way an individual head does. Non-communication among the members of a group head is the same thing as schizophrenia in an individual head. That goes for this group. This here college is a group head. This here state and country is a group head.

*Q: You talked a little about psychology and Buddhism. I'd like to hear more about that.*

In Buddhist psychology it's six senses, not five. It's the same five we have plus the sense of thought, which is perceived with the organ of the brain. And that the Buddhists group thought that way is very meaningful in their cosmology.

Now an example of somebody who's hung up in a sense is a voyeur. Well, a voyeur is somebody who's so far out into eye they'd rather look at it than do it. That's being way out into the eye sense, so

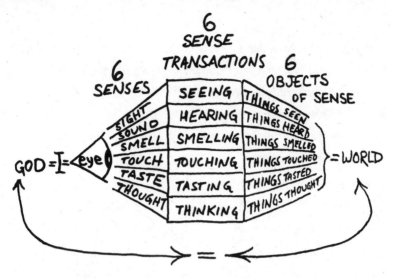

that the eye sense has become enormously magnified and the touch sense has become atrophied.

There's a piece of the human mind that you can look at in Freudian-Havelock Ellis kind of deep sexual weird terms that they do in Western psychology and say, "What a weird cat, man." But in Buddhist psychology you can look at him and you say, "Well, you've got to tune the eyeball back a little bit, and come out into touch some, and all that'll cool out."

Now you can see how that works for the five senses that you already know about … how you can get out into any one of them. A person can get into taste so heavy that he doesn't care that he wrecks his health and gets to weigh five hundred pounds and ruins his bod and might die in ten years, because he's riding taste so hard. All you've got to do is be a little ways out into a sense and it starts blowing the other ones.

Well what do you have to blow to get so far into taste that you eat yourself to death? Obviously you're not smart. It means you must've retracted your thought. See? That's the advantage of having thought hooked on that continuum, so you know how that works. Now here's the thing about thought: This culture doesn't know that thought is a sense. It thinks that thought is "I." And so in this culture they give you brownie points for braining all the time. You know, you get A's on your papers for running through all those mental masturbations that you run through—term papers, rat torturing, and you get points for going out into brain so far that you lose compassion, right? If you can torture rats to death for the sake of thought, you must have lost compassion somewhere along the line. Braining all the time isn't necessarily cool, any more than smelling all the time isn't necessarily cool.

The next thing they get to in Buddhist psychology is a group of eighteen things they group together, and what they are are the six senses, the six sense transactions, and the six objects of sense.

Now you come to a far out kind of an idea here. They teach that the object of meditation is the realization that the knower, the act of knowing, and the knowledge are all one. And that's kind of an interesting thing because that implies that the senses, the transactions, and the objects are all one, too.

Now the thing I teach, roughly, is the care, feeding, cleaning and manipulation of the universe/self system. And I don't have much of a 1-2-3 list or anything like that. I'm not as orderly as the Buddhists. I had to learn that great great thing—that we're all one. But knowing that, the universe is wide open.

*Q: In your diagram of the whole system, how is God defined, as the energy of the universe or the universe itself?*

The whole. The overall total whole.

*Q: ... Okay. Are you saying it's a conscious entity?*

Sometimes some of it is. This part, for instance, is really conscious. See, we are some of God being conscious. Everything I say to you, everything you say to anybody, everything anybody ever says to anybody is God talking to Himself.

*Q: ... Okay. Then it isn't necessary to forcefully integrate yourself into a universal pattern. You know what I mean.*

Right. You don't have to put yourself into an arbitrary universal pattern, but there is a normal way that the energy works, which … I use the word *karma*. I don't like to use words out of the language, I'm not much of a great one for italics and stuff, but I use *karma* because we don't have a word in English that means that quite well enough. Here's the way you have to write *karma* in English: *cause and effect*. In English we break those apart like they're somehow separate, but they're not. They're like space/time. They're that kind of a trip. They're not separate at all. Now cause/effect is just the wiring diagram of how it works, that what you put out you obviously get back.

*Q: … It seems redundant. "I" and Ego. That's not clear to me. You're saying that …*

Oh, you're worried about is that a self-other. That's good of you to catch that, but dig, here's how it really is: "I" is nothing but a focus point. See? The viewpoint's nothing but the focus point of these senses and has no other identity.

*Q: … You talked about getting too far into one of these senses. Well, where's the karma of why someone goes that far?*

Why do they do that? Now that is specifically what sin is about. I discovered what sin was from a couple of clues. Something that happened to me while I was stoned made me wonder about why I saw people who looked funny to me … whose eyes were open outrageous … looked like the biggest thing in their manifestation.

I saw that kind of stuff, and I'd been reading something in Aldous Huxley about a saint named Anselm. Saint Anselm was said to have figured out a system of penances for the confessors which would work on the five senses. He was working on a Western civilization five-sense model, and he said you could have sins scaled in seriousness from one to five.

You have five senses, you get a grand slam twenty-five if you really did the thing. And you work out the scale of how many Hail

Mary's and whatnot according to how serious an offense it was ... how many senses involved and all that. That's what that was, and it was in response to the idea that a feedback-loop into a sense is what a sin is. And like you go into a sense and you start caring about what's in that one and you get concerned about it to an unhealthy extent.

Q: *Are we in the end times?*

I don't really believe in that kind of thing. I've been into Buddhist psychology, because Zen seems the cleanest thing I've seen. Zen is so clean and so precise and pretty and just holy and compassionate. I really enjoy it a lot that way.

I think everybody really knows where it's at all the time and that the only handhold we in the here and now have on the future is to be groovy in the here and now. So what I teach is how to be groovy in the here and now by understanding the situation so you can work with it intelligently.

Now that's spiritual, you know. Spiritual isn't like misty or somewhere else. Spiritual is how do we, here and now, work it out as best we can, because this is all we have. The best place of course is to be neither liberal nor conservative. Being liberal or conservative, either one, is less energy than the possibility. Like if you're squirting a garden hose and it goes a certain distance, and you say you want it to go farther so you raise its angle up higher to make it go farther, but if you raise the angle up too high it starts coming back, right? That's just how a garden hose works.

Well, this is what was known by the philosophers of old as the Golden Mean, because it gets the most distance of anything. That's why the Golden Mean's heavy, because it does the job. It carries the mail. Like here's ways how conservative and liberal types could relate to a model like this: This here fellow is a liberal who says, "Oh, I'm afraid to aim too high. I may not be very good," you know, so he just dribbles out before he gets there. And this fellow here says, "I'm going to aim for the very, very highest, man," and blows his juice out before he gets there. So the Golden Mean in conjunction with the senses model are good tools to help you keep sane. That's shorthand, but I hope it's understood.

Recognize no Buddha outside yourself. The Buddhists say, "If somebody says Buddha, stop your ears," you know, don't start a self-other relationship with the universe at all.

There's only one Church, it's the material plane, and everybody on the planet is a member of it. You don't need to hang anything around your neck, your bellybutton does it all. That's your membership button in that Church. There's only One, and it's like how do the monkeys do the monkeys, and if the monkeys don't do the monkeys right, that isn't the One.

*Q: Can you make somebody feel better by just doing tantra on a vibrational level?*

Yeah. You can heal anybody a lot just by doing that. But here's the thing about the way uptightness works: Uptightness has kind of a decimal scale to it, because a person can be uptight and say, "Well I can't face this right now," and squish that whole uptightness into a little brick and stash it.

And then something else comes along and makes them uptight and they can take that whole uptightness and kind of stash it and forget it. Then when they go to relax what they do is they say, "Whew, now I'm relaxed," except they still have four bricks of uptightness over here they haven't relaxed yet. They've got to take those bricks out, unwrap them, whoosh, fills you up with uptightness, relax that one, take out that other brick, open it up, accept it, and relax that one, and you've got to go all the way back through your transactions, anywhere you got uptight, and relax each one.

See, that's what your evening meditation is supposed to be, knowing every transaction that happened to you all day long and relaxing

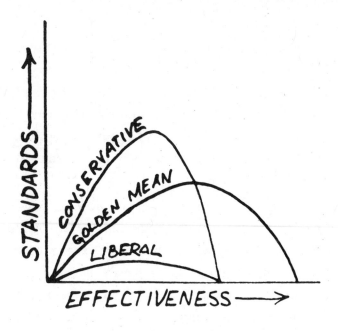

the uptightness out of it. And if you do that your health will stay good and you'll get smarter and go toward enlightenment and that kind of thing. And you don't like have to sit up to do this kind of a meditation. You can do that as you're lying in your bed, just the last thing before you go to sleep.

*Q: I'd like you to explain the kind of meditation you do.*

Well, I do several. What I'm sitting in now is kind of like the Oriental meditation position. I'm not sitting up very straight, I could do that a little better. You're supposed to keep your back straight and all that. That's an oriental meditation position. Kneeling on your knees—like you do in a church, where they have a little knee rail there, and you kneel down and all that—straightens your back the same way, and kneeling is Christian meditation position, except Christians call their meditation prayer.

Now in Egypt they have those pictures of the throne of the pharaohs—great big high-backed thing and arms up like this. That's the Egyptian meditation position is sitting up in that kind of a chair with your back straight. Well, we do one that we've been doing for a while, which we haven't done much lately because we've been so busy doing an engagement every other day or so, but when we're in San Francisco we do a Sunday Morning Service every Sunday morning and we do it standing, which is another way of keeping your back straight, and we meet about half an hour, forty-five minutes before sunrise and face which way the sun's going to come from and watch it go through its changes in silence, standing together, and get higher and higher and higher.

Usually by the time the sun cracks over the edge we're really stoned, and when the sun comes over the edge we OM together for a while. And anybody anywhere who wanted to have a kind of a meeting where you could be with other people and have communion and not be afraid of having your mind copped could agree with a bunch of people to meet on some hilltop and do that, and nobody would have to be a preacher or anything even.

Now in a meditation, when you pacify your body first and then while you try to get your head together, thoughts are going to come through your head that are going to be a hassle to you, and it's going to be, "What am I doing here," or "Somebody really put the blocks to me yesterday, I really felt bad about that," or something you think you did wrong, or worrying about, "I forgot to pay that parking ticket," whatever. Well, all that stuff that's kind of like garbage that comes up in your head is your subconscious, and that's the meditation is meeting that stuff and taking care of it, which is looking at it and saying, "Parking ticket, pay the thing next time you see it," or, "Did I blow it yesterday, who cares, forget it."

And clean up your head until you can stand there and actually get serious, which may take you twenty-five minutes or so, and you get to where you can get actually serious, where you can look at the sun coming up and you can start thinking about things like the sun being the giver of all life to the planet, all the energy we use—like coal is just somebody else's sun, but still sun, just stored in the ground … oil, whatnot.

Realize that we're all one, that what you do to your brother you do to yourself, and mainly, as you sow, so you shall reap. And if you can get to a serious place of mind and think about that stuff and then realize what it's like, you can realize its full value. Truth can become an old proverb and an old saw and everybody's heard that a million times and it doesn't have any weight in it, but in a meditation place you can go to a place where that stuff has its full value and you realize that it's the bread of life. Just talking about how you could get serious and get real makes me feel very stoned with you right now.

*Q: You seem to be relatively optimistic about the future.*

I try not to be optimistic or pessimistic. I try just to handle the thing that's in front of me. I'm in favor of affecting it rather than having opinions about it.

*Q: There seems to be among people with a gift of prophecy a rather widespread belief that during the future there's going to be a fantastic amount of destruction, maybe even total destruction. Do you have any feelings about that?*

Well I'll tell you, I think that prophets of destruction should probably have stayed in bed and kept their mouths shut. I don't even believe in that kind of prophecy anyway.

*Q: Would you describe your family life? Are there rules and regulations like in a monastic order?*

No, not so much like that … except that if you be on the Caravan, we make it day to day by how cool we be, and if you don't be as cool as us so you make it dangerous for us, then you've got to shape up. And then along that line is that the Caravan is a traveling monastery, if you like, in that it's a religious thing I'm trying to teach all the time.

Well, the way I teach is I tell everybody what I see when I see it, and we just go ahead and do what we're going to do—move the buses, you know, go ahead and do a thing, and they let me kind of walk around unmolested and tell them what I see. As far as like structure or family life goes, I feel that like the shape or structure of your family life isn't what's so important so long as it's a real compassion and commitment thing.

Nobody has ever seen me hard-ass a cop, for instance. And anybody who watches me for a minute learns the way I do that and they know how to do that, sort of by example. Also I have been giving lecture things for a long time. This is a telepathic phenomenon. I get the use of the group head when we're all together here like this.

Like you guys are letting me use this group head. This is a fine group head. It's a smart one and I knew it was heavy during the OM, it felt strong, and I enjoyed getting to talk about this kind of stuff. Sometimes I can't talk about this. Sometimes the highest level of discourse I can reach is, "Everybody get together and love one another right now."

Room full of schoolteachers is a certain kind of group head. A bunch of schoolteachers come to take a class on drugs, because that's happening so outrageously all over the country and they want to know, "What's this about? Is this just the absolute decadence of all moral structure? What is this that seems to be going on, because some people say they find God and other people seem to be flipping out and going nuts?"

And then a schoolteacher has a certain area of interest. I used to be an elementary schoolteacher, and I taught in San Francisco State College, and there's a thing ... if you're a real teacher at all you see kids in plain interaction—monkey to monkey—in front of you all the time doing their thing, and you notice how they do it, and because they do it a little subtler around you because you're the schoolteacher, perhaps, doesn't mean that that isn't the game they do, and you get to know the kids.

So the question that comes up about drugs, then, is what does it do to people and how does it make them be, because you see how people be and you see what little things can make them change if you've been paying attention. Well, I'm assuming that you've been teaching school and paying attention. Am I talking to the right folks? What you want to know about is what does it do to the monkey, really.

I've been in San Francisco for about five years watching the community, meeting with fifteen hundred people each Monday night and being able to monitor a rather large statistical percentage of the psychedelic population of the world. I've been able to watch people over a period of five years and I have some better statistics, I think, actually,

*89*

on what the effects of drugs are on the mind than pretty much anybody else. The scientific method, as used in the laboratory, has hampered the medical world from getting an accurate idea of the nature of drugs.

What I've found is that, as anywhere else, if you keep your wits together and if you work at it and if you try hard and pay attention, that psychedelics can be used for growth. I don't think we need speed, heroin, or barbiturates. I don't find growth in those; I find regression. But we didn't mainly come out to talk about drugs. What we mainly came out to talk about was peace.

We're still operating on the teachings of Jesus and Buddha as concerning violence, and are able to travel at all because of that. What we came out for is to come on to people and say, We aren't scary, we didn't go crazy, and here we are, and we're interested in Spirit and we're interested in getting the planet together, starting from the closest thing around us, like making a human contact with the first person sitting in front of you.

If he happens to be a police officer writing you a ticket, your job is still to make a human contact with him, forgive him for any inconvenience. That's an outrageous thing, you know. Some folks think I'm weird because I can't dig killing a cop. There's a whole piece of this culture that thinks it's a sin to spank a child but that it's okay to shoot a cop. I think that's an interesting sort of equation there, too. I think that we're in the kickback of indulgent child raising, which has been popular in the past.

Now I've talked enough that you've got some idea of where I'm at. I've taken a lot of psychedelics, but I don't have to be shown the splendors of the universe any more times to make me know they're real. I don't have to be given that vision any more times to know it's real because I see it all the time now. So what I'd like to do from here is questions and answers.

*Q: Do you think you would have found the splendors of the universe without psychedelics?*

Rocking Jody Morning Star used to say that LSD is a rocket ship and peyote is an ox cart but it's only a mile to town. You could even walk.

I have no way of knowing that from here. All I can say is that I was along into middle life and hadn't heard of them as yet. Somehow or other I got that standard American Christmas card education about religion that didn't have any juice in it, and I didn't know that there was anything heavy or had been heavy, and psychedelics were the first thing that attracted my attention from the time I was about three years old and decided that I had it figured out.

If you can get your mother snowed when you're a year old so you have her rigged, you don't have to grow emotionally from then on. You can grow physically and chronologically and not grow emotionally at all, just so your getting-things machine is honed down fine enough that you have your mother trained. There are people walking around all over the streets, emotionally one, two, three, four, five years old, whatever place they managed to do that at, if they did that.

*Q: I don't know if I have the expression right, but you said at one time in talking about psychedelics that you used them in teaching religion. … Well then, how do you use them to teach religion?*

Okay. That's a good question, thank you. Jesus taught that what they call the hereafter or other world or Spirit world or something like that was not something that was far away but was immediate. He said, "The Kingdom is at hand." He didn't mean that it was going to happen any minute, he meant right there. What he calls the Kingdom is what the Japanese Zen Buddhists call Buddha's Pure Western Land.

Now there are several ways that you can attain to Nirvana. You can do like a purely intellectual method where you come to understand the nature of the universe in its truthfulness till you see how everything works, and then you're at peace with the universe because you see everything following its laws. To be peaceful, you don't want to change anything because you understand how it works and you're willing to work with how it works. This is the Jewel in the Lotus, the attainment of Nirvana.

Now most of the religious teachings of the world are about ways to prepare yourself to develop enough moral character so that if it ever gets heavy for you, somehow or other you'll make the straight-on, strong human decisions that'll stone you, and that's why they're teaching moral structure from the very earliest thing.

Now we're in a time of low moral structure, I have to say. I'm fairly liberal in a lot of places, but I think we're too far out into pornography and sadism and that kind of thing. I don't like to see the kind of stuff I'm seeing in movies, television, that kind of business, terrible stuff actually. That stuff on the television is a product of our national subconscious.

With psychedelics you can see the workings of that world—the subconscious—you can see the figure-ground shift. Most of what we see is an agreement of what we pay attention to as being important and the other stuff we don't pay attention to as being unimportant.

For instance, this room is in your subconscious and as such looks a certain way. That means that you take this room for granted. You be here all the time, this is the room you always meet in, you're kind of used to it. It's a plain old room, so you're not paying any attention to it. From a stoned viewpoint the room comes on to me rather science-fiction-y and a little like 2001 … pretty spacey actually. A funny way to arrange monkeys. That's an example of a kind of perception.

Someone who smokes cigarettes, for instance, has subconscious habit patterns because that's the only way you can smoke cigarettes is that—if you're going to smoke twenty a day or so—you develop subconscious habit patterns. That stuff stands out to the eye that is seeing the subconscious—those habit-run gestures.

You can see to the point of flat-out telepathy what's going on in another person's mind. You can see their aura and know from what color their aura is what their emotional temperament is. Sometimes you can see little pictures floating around their head with pictures of their thought content in it.

I was high one time with a fellow who just had a new girlfriend who he was just really mind-blown over, really enamored of completely, and we were sitting together looking at each other and enjoying the hallucinations, which is like reading each other's minds—it's pretty stoned in here now too—and I saw a bunch of little pictures around his head which were shaped like television things, round corners except some triangular and some oblong and whatnot, little things around his head, and there was a picture running inside each one. In one picture she was leaning back unsnapping her bra, and in another picture she was just getting out of the bath, and all that kind of thing, and his head was full of these pictures of his new lady, and I could look into his mind like that and see his most intimate things, thinking about being with his lady.

Well, some people see that sort of thing and think that they're the only one that sees that, and that tends to drive them crazy sometimes, because they see what's in people's heads, and you see outrageous stuff sometimes in people's heads because there's lots of very nice folks carrying very Freudian subconscious, which to that eye is really visible, and you get a sixteen-year-old with the eye of the teacher—the ability to see men's souls—walking down skid row looking at the souls, and he freaks out.

That's one of the ways people can freak out. Or a couple of people who think they know each other come on together and look at each other and see that they don't know each other at all and say, "What am I doing here with you? Who are you anyway?" … also can happen.

I took a lot of psychedelics. I didn't have much happen about the first five times, and about the sixth time I had a white light experience, which was the ecstasy trip that they talk about. White light and bodily ecstasy. But I didn't learn anything from it. But somewhere

along the line it got to where it wasn't freaky, and it wasn't strange, and it wasn't a weird trip anymore. It was just like seeing where people were really at, and I found that if I came on to somebody where they were really at, as I could see it, that I could make their subconscious conscious, which is to perform the act that a priest is supposed to perform in confession, or that a psychiatrist is supposed to perform in therapy.

In either case it makes people sane. And people who learn how to do that together have been accumulating more and more since then so that there's thousands of us actually now who really understand how that kind of thing works, and who are doing our best to try to make all of us sane faster, so that we can get the group head of the nation saner faster, because it's a little nutty in spots. Enlightenment is much like sanity, or being a grownup. You see, this is a special kind of a group head in here. This is really a special kind of a group head because there's that air of responsibility place—"What are you doing to the kids?" You know. I really feel that in the air, just zzzzzzzt, strong.

*Q: Do you think that enlightenment could happen to a person who's not on a psychedelic?*

Oh, all the time. It could happen to you while you're making love, for instance. You know how they used to talk about there was something really magical about the shared orgasm and then it became fashionable to say, "Oh well, what's the difference." But there is something really magical about the shared orgasm, and it can be satori—the transmission of mind, just like from a Zen Patriarch to a Zen Patriarch—it can be just that between lovers.

That's what some of the heavy juice behind the great lover thing is about. There is magic in love, right in there, because it's an ego death. A mutual orgasm is an ego death because both parties have got to let go of their ego or it can't happen. So long as one of them is holding on, it's one of those sexual rip-offs where somebody loses.

*Q: What do you think about bad trips?*

I think that that is people being shown into pieces of their subconscious that they don't want to look at, admit is theirs, or cop to. I've had them, you know. My first hundred trips I never had a bad trip, and I was over at this cat's house telling him how I never had a bad trip and he talked me into tripping at his house and ambushed and just wasted me. He spent a couple of hours chasing me through my rationalizations and out of my ego defenses. And I had a bad trip, man, it just really blew my mind.

It was really good for me. It was the most intensely painful thing that happened to me in my whole life up to that time, but it was so good for me, it really straightened me up. It was a bear at the time, but I have to admit that I remember it with warm affection and even a smile.

I have to say that I dig all those places where it got heavy because in every one of them I was forced to learn something to survive, and as such the things I learned are so precious. Sometimes I feel that I've been using my old tool out of my toolbox, all worn down and sharp on the edge, and I know where I got it. For instance on that trip that I just mentioned I learned about non-attachment, and that's such a precious jewel.

*Q: Is your group in any way politically oriented?*

Basically I'm interested in enlightenment. I figure if people are sane and enlightened, they'll make the right choices. On the other hand, we dare not ignore politics.

*Q: May I ask a question? In your philosophy can't an individual lose his identity and become one of the group, and can't this have certain consequences?*

I don't know what you mean by "certain consequences."

*Q: Well, if there's some end result to it, okay, because generally most movements are working towards some end goal.*

We're not goal-directed.

*Q: … Then what is your reason for existing?*

The deluding passions are infinite. I vow to extinguish them all. Sentient beings are numberless. I vow to save them all. The way of the Buddha is unattainable. I vow to attain it. The laws of the dharma are impossible to expound. I vow to expound them all.

*Q: … Okay, and what would this bring if it came about?*

No, wait a minute. You hear all those unattainable and impossible and all that? What do you mean, "came about?" They can't come about. I just have this oar. I'm so happy to have a handle to pull on that I'll just sit here and pull on it.

*Q: … Then you'll never reach it but you'll be moving towards it?*

I don't know, but I'm not attached at that place. I got things to do here right now. Like I've got to come to an agreement right here with you about what we're talking about. That's the handle I have to the universe right now. So that's the piece of the universe I'm interacting with.

Sometimes when I'm driving our school bus I'm steering the universe right down the road. I've got my body politic on, eleven foot high, fourteen thousand pounds, eight foot wide, going down the road, and I'm steering the universe, and I'm making decisions, right and wrong.

That's what you should do. See, that's what we're doing here now. It's not goal-directed. It's taking care of business as you go along. Mankind's been around for a long time. We are going to continue around for a long time more. We do have to go another hundred and twenty-six million years to prove we were as good as the dinosaurs.

This is a Catholic school, I believe. I see Jesus Christ on the wall down there. How many people here have a firm belief in religion and that there is something besides the material plane that we must in some way or another deal with, would you raise your hand just to see? Far out ... that's a fantastic miracle because when I was in school you couldn't get that agreement. There wouldn't have been but ten or twenty people that would have admitted to the existence of Spirit.

At first I thought that I was going to invent new systems about how to get it together because we needed to get it together. So I started off thinking about what I was going to do, and as my calculations grew, I had to start including factors such as that people who lived a long time ago were just as smart as people who live right now. We didn't suddenly just become smart last week. The minds of the philosophers and teachers of thousands of years ago were just as alert, just as sharp, just as attuned to the subtleties of the universe as any scientist or philosopher that lives today ... at least.

When you come on stoned, the first thing you see is that if morality had been abstract to you previously, it suddenly becomes right there in front of you, because it's your bread of life. If you be wrong your energy goes down, and you can be wrong till your energy goes down so far that you can terminate your contract.

So I started thinking of all the things you'd have to do to set up something that would be really straight, that every monkey could trust. I thought that a real religion would have to affirm the essential oneness of all of them. I found that later expressed in Mahayana Buddhism and the infinite love of the Christ. I found as I studied other religions that all religions were put together by somebody some time or other with exactly those same criteria in mind—that it be all-inclusive, that it be fair. It's that Buddha's Universal Church and the Catholic Church are the same.

I didn't always have such pure high religious ideals. In fact I didn't used to have any at all. I got into religion in the early days of the hip thing in San Francisco, and I had experiences that convinced me that religion was real and that what I had thought was an empty morality structure was a description of how the universe works.

Now I can talk about anything actually, and maybe the best way to get on with the meeting is to find out what do we need to know here and now? Try me out, ask me anything.

*Q: What if you come up on a guy whose head is in the same place as yours is, are you in the same world or is it your world and his world?*

If I come up to somebody whose head is in the same place that my head is in, what I usually do is really love them a lot, and they really love me a lot, and we say, "Far out." Right then you're in the same world. That's a good question.

*Q: How do you think that living the way you have has benefited your-self and others?*

When we got to Yellowstone we found out some of us were on welfare, so we said that everybody who was on welfare had to quit and take care of themselves. So that money is there available for anybody who really needs it. And being vegetarian helps there to be more food on the planet. Living collectively is more economical and makes more to go around in a world were resources are drying up.

*Q: How do you finance your Caravan?*

Some folks have been raking leaves, some folks have been painting houses, some have been picking pumpkins. When I said it was a working Caravan, the folks that were on welfare had to start working, because when we're rolling it costs three hundred dollars a day in gasoline alone to move the Caravan all day. We're working and moving the Caravan and we're building up the engines and keeping them together and towing buses and accepting new people on top of all that, for no other reason than to go out in the world and say that Spirit is where it's at and that love is heavier than violence.

*Q: I like all this, but it seems to me I've heard it before in every religion I've studied and I've studied a lot of different religions.*

Thank you.

*Q: How are you going to decide on which is the one truth? You said it's yours, somebody else said it was his.*

No, I don't say it's mine. I'm just borrowing it. It's been hanging around for thousands and thousands of years, and I just picked it up and nobody seemed to respect it. I thought it was a nice thing, so I've been trying to make respect for it around where I am, and it's the same one. In Minneapolis the arrangement to speak was made by a Methodist minister, and we spoke in a Catholic church. I teach Christianity and Zen Buddhism and Judaism and Sufism, just for a start.

The people that have come with me are not sorted on national background, they're all kinds of colors, and they came from all kinds of different religious structures, and they can all say that there is that one pure note that goes through them all and that's what we're seeking. We're uniting folks together and we're doing things, and if you want to know how to do it and what to do, watch us because we're doing it.

*Q: When you tripped in the early times, did you feel like there was a question that was just hanging there and you didn't know what the question was?*

Yeah.

*Q: ... I was wondering if you still felt ...*

Uh-uh. In my early trips I used to feel like I had a black box in my head and I couldn't look inside. I knew all of my whole trip except inside that box and I didn't know what was in there, and I wanted to know what it was. I don't feel that at all anymore. It's like when I taught a student that she didn't have to be paranoid about being constipated—what goes in will come out in time. Well, I found out my head was like that and it's no mystery anymore.

*Q: ... What was in the little black box?*

What was in the little black box was I was afraid to die. When I found that out, I wasn't afraid to die anymore, then that was the little black box, and I never had a little black box since then. For a while I was really afraid. I used to worry about it and sweat it. Then it got to where I didn't worry about that anymore.

When I say that I'm not afraid of death, I mean I have no continuing concern about it. That is not to say that I don't look both ways before I step off the curb, and if you came and tried to kill me, you would find an old ex-Marine fighting seriously dirty.

But I am not sitting around worrying about death catching up with me.

*Q: What are your feelings on the concept of the collective unconscious?*

I don't so much have feelings on the concept of the collective unconscious, but I kind of swamp around in it in my hip boots every now and then. People are always coming to me with their weird problems, which they're convinced are absolutely unique and which I always recognize as yet more manifestations of the collective unconscious coming up here. I try to make it conscious. Making the subconscious conscious makes you free—releases you of bad karma, makes you get healthy and helps you get smarter.

*Q: How can you be sure that telling the truth is the proper thing to do at the time and that people will know it's right?*

You have to make a decision on the basis of your own judgment, with the possibility that you may make a mistake. That's the only kind of decision that's worthwhile. That's the only time when you exert your free will. You have to make decisions and decide to do something every now and then ... even if it seems to be heavy. That's all I'm doing: I'm just making decisions on my own free will to decide to do a bunch of stuff because I think it needs to be done.

*Q: I'm having trouble getting something straight. That is, one part of me says that I should not kill anybody at any time under any circumstances. Another part of me, perhaps my childhood training, says that I should be able to kill in self-defense.*

The way that comes out to me is that you should be able to defend yourself. Taking of life should be the absolutely last option. I've made that choice. You've got to make that choice too, and if we all make it then it's not even scary or dangerous to make that choice. It's only scary when you're the first one.

*Q: I see one of the problems of traditional religion being that people interpret Jesus saying, "I am the way," to mean, "I am the only way."*

Right. That's a heavy point.

*Q: ... How do you deal with that? How do you keep the people on your Caravan from saying that you are the only religion or you are the only way?*

I don't let them, for one thing. Jesus said, "There's no way to the Father but through me." Well, when Jesus said "me," most of the time he didn't mean Jesus—he meant the Christ function. That was his "I"— his "I" was single. That meant that his universal "I" and his personal pronoun were the same one. So when he said, "There's no way to the Father but through me," he was speaking of himself as Christ consciousness, not as individual single personal dude Jesus. A lot of people get hung up thinking the only way through is through historical Jesus. When Jesus said that, he meant Christ consciousness, and Christ consciousness persists in all times in all ages ... and under other names.

*Q: Do you feel this is true of all religions, that the leaders of the great religions did not feel that all people had to believe in just that person?*

I don't think Jesus meant that from in front. I think he got kind of institutionalized. Buddha made it very plain. He said that there have been Buddhas for eternity and will be Buddhas on for eternity, and that you should take no refuge outside yourself, so they didn't get hung up on him personally so bad. He made it plain that you've got to make your own decision, do your own thing.

It's really stoned in here. It feels good, feels like spring water. Thank you very much and God Bless you, and thank you for letting us be here. Good night.

*We went to Goddard, and picked up Martin Pear from there who was study-*
*ing community in college and quit just before graduation to come with us on*
*the Caravan because he saw we were a community passing through.*

GODDARD COLLEGE
PLAINFIELD, VERMONT
22 NOVEMBER 1970

The way I did class in San Francisco is I'd just take off blowing this horn and we'd all OM together for a while, it being a good way to integrate a bunch of heads into a head. Since I've been on the road I've found it's best to talk a little bit to get the subconscious conscious so we all know some of the same things before we get into that, and then it makes the OM come on stronger when we do it.

What we're here for now is communion, just flat out. Ain't here to talk politics, ain't here to do rock and roll. Just communion. Now to get to communion we've got to get to some kind of an agreement on all the planes before we can get so fancy and flossy as to come to high spiritual communion. We got to be checked out on the other levels before we get there so we know where we're at and what we're doing. Now the folks here at this school ought to know something about what a group head is because you be of this little bitty group head out in the boondocks here by yourselves.

It seems that the rules of sanity for a group head work the same way as they do for an individual. Non-communication among the members of the group head is the same thing as schizophrenia in an individual. So the idea here is to get some together. Now we came out from San Francisco because we felt like we were some together. We wanted to come around and bring that around the country, and we have hopes of doing that here for you, with you, around you, however. But to get to that, we've got to get to where we're supposed to be, and we haven't had any meetings much for a while of the kind where we do homework and take care of business. We've been taking care of Dayton, Ohio's business and Ann Arbor, Michigan's business and other places' business. Well, we're going to do a little bit of our own business and then go on and get high from there.

Now I'm supposed to be a religious teacher. As such I'm supposed to teach about karma, so I'll tell you a little story about my latest brush with karma so you may understand the kind of karma I'm talking about. Way back about five or six weeks ago we left San Francisco. When we got up to Oregon we had a big brush with the heat and they were afraid we were carrying bombs and guns and whatnot and checked us out right close.

We had a good encounter with them, good enough that we had a protective umbrella of police teletype which carried us the rest of the way across the western states. So we came along running on good police teletype into Minneapolis and down into Iowa. Michigan State Police radioed ahead to the Ohio State Police. Everybody loved us. Coming up out of Ohio we'd been doing a lot of hard work and we'd been out rolling and we hit the Canadian border and the Canadians didn't want us, them having their own troubles.

I was disappointed about that, which is one of the things that happens to you when you get appointed is the risk of disappointment. So I came on just a taste to the head of the Canadian immigration and leaned on him just a little bit to see if he'd let us in. I suspect I wasn't compassionate with Canada's internal troubles at that time because they didn't feel like being leaned on and he cut me loose from the head of the Caravan and shipped me back across the border and held the rest of the Caravan over in Canada for a short time while he took everybody's name and checked them out.

We got separated from the Caravan. We have about twenty-five buses here, and we have a total of fifty. The rest are scattered out somewhere across New York State, Vermont, and Ohio. We know where a few of them are: valve job in Ann Arbor, a new engine in Detroit, new engine in Davenport. So we came scattered across the rest of Ohio and Pennsylvania and we came into New York, and the next encounter we had with the heat was crossing the New York state line. We started finding out what was happening—that we didn't have any good teletype out in front of us anymore. Somewhere along the line Canada didn't put out quite as good a report on us as we'd been having all along, which was probably because I'd hard-assed the Canadian head of immigration just a taste. So we didn't have very good telex when we hit the edge of New York State.

We were going along, and this police car pulls up beside me and runs me off down this dirt road on the side. I get out and walk over to the police car and say, "Hi! This the way to New York City?"

He says, "No. Got any dope?" And I learned a couple of lessons about the wisdom of the way I run my mouth around the police.

They asked me and I lied—for incredibly complex karmic reasons (chickened out). I wasn't as on top as I could have been when I said to the cop that I didn't have any grass. I was scratching. I was doing the best I could do, but I knew where I'd blown it, and I knew where the karma began for that whole trip, because that karma began back at the Canadian border when I was a little tired and it was too much trouble for me to come up on top and give the Canadian border guard the best one I had. And I let in a hole in my bucket then.

Fortunately the folks that had been running with me for a while kept their wits about them better than I did and managed to come through New York with good karma. Having been asked if they had grass, they said yes. They got busted and paid twenty-five dollar fines in New York State for grass. And now we have good telex again because it's back on the teletype that we tell the truth, even though I didn't—everybody else did. So we got a quorum up anyhow.

Most good of you to carry me over in that place.

Now that's about karma and about cause and effect—about as ye sow so ye shall reap. Right? Now we understand karma real well, and we make it across the United States by how we do our karma. We see hundreds of cops every day, and that many see us too because none of them look at us and miss us, you know. It's not that they don't notice.

Now that brings it around to where I haven't got any subconscious with this group, so I can now talk to this group how I want to. I can tell you what I see now because I'm up even with you, because we're all knowing the same things about us now. Now let's start off from here and OM a bit.

Jesus said that the Kingdom is at hand. When he said that, he did not mean just about to happen, gonna happen in a day or two, just a minute, or anything like that—he meant at hand, here and now, right here. Now the reason I bring that up is because it's relevant to why I put up with so much trouble for the sake of grass. I was raised in a materialist culture, the culture of the United States—same one you were raised in mostly. A few of you may have had some kind of a real religious upbringing, but most of you didn't. The reason I bring up the question of grass is because it was the first thing in my life that led me to put any credence in anything spiritual.

As I've said before, I managed to go through and get a Master's degree in creative writing without ever finding out that the statements about Spirit by people like William Blake and John Donne were statements about Spirit, and not just mere poetic metaphors. And it was my experience with psychedelics which showed me that there was and is another plane of experience other than the material plane which is with us all the time. And if we don't be faithful to that other plane, the material plane will fall apart and turn to crap on us.

Now modern science teaches you that matter is first and anything else must descend from matter. Some modern scientists will even cop to telepathy, but they say it's a function of the material plane, not that it's a function of the spiritual plane on the way to the material. Jesus was asked which came first, the material plane or the spiritual plane, and he said, "I marvel not that everything depends on Spirit, I only marvel that so much riches can have its home in such poverty." And he meant by that that we who are only different from a lump of dung by a minor chemical change can be a repository for Spirit, called whatever name from whatever culture that you care to call it—same thing.

Now I have to go back to another karmic place and tell you how come we came out here on the road at all. It's what you call a calling. I think what a calling is is being just naturally schizy enough to perceive vibrations and know there's something else going on. In fact the classical enlightenment path is schizophrenia. That's that place where it says, "If you can, when you're in the dark night of the soul, call on me, I will come and be with you," and means that if you go stone crazy to that weird psychedelic-looking place, that if you can come on not for yourself but for mankind, and if you can ask for help humbly and honestly from that place, that you can figure-ground it out to enlightenment. You can be crazy or enlightened depending on what kind of trip you're having. If you're having a good trip, if it's good enough, you're enlightened. If you're having a bummer, you're just another one having a bummer.

Now, we stake our whole way of being on the idea that the spiritual plane is the progenitor of the material plane.

We put our faith in a clean universe.

It's kind of a funny thing for us to be talking at universities and colleges at all, because I don't know why anybody's going to a university or a college, because they aren't where it's at. The only way I can really understand this place here is as being some kind of really expensive commune that your parents pay for. It seems to me that if this commune had to make it on its own horsepower and your parents weren't paying for it, that it would probably collapse. That's a funny kind of commune to live in. See, this is why I had to go and get straight with you at the very beginning. I had in mind that I was going to say this kind of thing down here, and I had to be cool.

It's good news that there's something you can do about the situation, and it's within your power to do it, and it makes a difference. What more can you ask for? Now everybody knows what straighten up means; everybody knows what cool and uncool means. I hear a lot of people haggle over the details.

Like straight means straighten up, you know, and cool means being cool, like loving your fellow human and resisting the temptation that I fell heir to in Canada to take a piece off his butt on the way past. Everybody knows that kind of stuff, since that's all part of the monkey rules. What I'd like to do is go on ahead and get into conversation with Goddard here and find out what's happening with you all, and we'll tell you what's happening with us. Just raise your hand and ask about anything at all.

*Q: Once I saw auras, but I quit because it freaked me out. I'm wondering how to use the power and how to develop it.*

Okay. Here's about how to see third-eye vision. How many people here have seen auras, raise your hands, would you? See, that's quite a few folks here who've seen auras. Let me try another thing. How many have been into seeing auras when you weren't on psychedelics, would you raise your hand? Oh, that's pretty good. Like it's really easy to see them when you're stoned.

Here's the thing, you can't let the power freak you out if you're going to use it, because you can see into men's souls. You can see right into people's souls. And if you can be compassionate and not revolted by anything you see so you can give people just, exact, unemotional information on the nature of their subconscious, you can help them become more sane. Sometimes when I'm talking to somebody and telling them what I see in their head, I see them get better-looking word by word as I hip them to it, just watch them across the board get prettier.

If you can help somebody's subconscious be conscious, that's bringing their soul out of hell. It's a heavy responsibility. Some people get a little bit of vision and go, "Oh yark! Everybody's so filthy." Well, you too, brother, all of us. We've all got a little funky subconscious here and there now and then, but it can be got out, if you've got friends you can trust. If you had the vision, you can have it again. It's a groove, you know. Go ahead and do it, but don't get hung up in it. The major thing is being on the money in the here and now. Don't go seeking psychic phenomena. Astral desires hang you up as bad as physical desires. Okay on that one? Somebody come on out front.

*Q: In the* Tibetan Book of the Dead *where it talks about ego loss, would you say a lot of people freak out because they can't accept this ego loss?*

Right, I think that's the only thing anybody ever freaks out over is because they can't accept ego loss. I don't think there's anything else that freaks you out. You can handle anything else except, "Oh my precious thing! You don't mean that one!" And the universe says, "Yeah, that's the one we want." You know, the universe don't want anything but all you got. And then you're cool if you can gracefully let go of it, but if you don't, it'll just slam you up against the wall a few times until you straighten up or get tired of tripping and come down and say, "Wow, that was a funny trip."

This paragraph was a blatant anthropomorphizing of the universe. It actually doesn't do any of those things.

*Q: Do you know why it happens to some people to get high completely spontaneously?*

I know lots of folks that are stoned on the natch, and it's a groovy thing, but the core of that question is if you never heard of being stoned, what would ever turn you on to try to do it? That's where I was at. If I'd ever heard of getting stoned any time previously to getting stoned, I would have got that way then.

*Q: What's busting your ego?*

You can't really bust it, you know. Your ego is your viewpoint, and if you lose it, you haven't got a viewpoint and you aren't in this plane anymore. That's called dying. When they say ego death it means your ego experiences what it's like to die, but you come back because it's not your time yet.

The thing about ego death is your ego comes right back as soon as it's killed. It comes right back, but if you take the care to keep it straight ... you can just watch what's going on out there and don't think about what's going on in here—don't think, "How am I doing," or, "Gee, I'm neat." If you take care of business out front, then you don't get into ego trouble, but if your ego, which is your viewpoint, gets into rear-view mirrors you get ego trouble, which ranges from, "Look at me, ain't I pretty," which is kind of naive ego, on out into, "I don't see anybody else but me," which is where you mistreat other people because you're so oblivious to anybody else.

Here's the thing about a rear-view mirror: It may show you the thing in back, but it also blots out that piece of the scenery that's behind the mirror. People can get so many mirrors stacked up that they ain't even seeing the scenery anymore. All they're seeing is themselves. That's a real ego problem.

Now psychedelics and truth and good friends and watching a baby born or watching somebody die or anything like that can bring you around to the realization that you aren't the only monkey on the planet. And if you can snap to the realization that you are not the only monkey on the planet, then you can get so you are not so obnoxious that you make it bad for the other monkeys. Then that's not having an ego problem.

Q: *How do you explain people who have reached enlightenment telling people who have not, not to indulge in sex?*

I didn't know that they did. I think I must say that it's beyond discussion. Sex is cool. You can have sex and get high. You can reach satori and enlightenment making love. Anybody who says that making love will specifically keep you from getting on doesn't understand the nature of monkeys.

I don't think there's anything to giving up sex, but I do think there's a thing to giving up lust and desire; I think lust and desire will hang you up. But people can have lust for ice cream that will hang them up. The thing that hangs you up is lust, and it doesn't matter whether it's for sex or ice cream or candy bars. They're not heavy at that level.

How about that? Like you don't know what to think about that, but did you hear it and understand the transmission? Ah-ha, thank you.

Q: *The thing I've read is the reason they go for no sex is because it takes up so much energy and you can use that energy for your enlightenment.*

Right, that is the reasoning behind anti-sex things. Part of it is to try to keep you out of trouble, because there's such a mess of emotional stuff you can fall into all around sex.

But if you're a yogi, you're supposed to get above all that emotional stuff anyway, whether or not you give up sex. So then the reason becomes a question of saving up energy. But you can make love in a way that does not expend energy. If you make love in the ordinary Western man-on-top position, and the man goes bang-bang-bang and gets his jollies like a Beethoven ending and the lady's still waiting, well, that's an energy-loss trip.

But if a man and a woman are really together and really move that energy back and forth between them, it gains instead of loses. You can take the energy that you start with making love and subtly, vibrationally push it back and forth, and it'll get you higher and higher and higher till it puts you right into the void, just flash you right out on just pure loving juice.

What your body is driving for when you have body sex desire is that you have a charge of a certain kind of energy, which is just like when the clouds are going overhead with positive charges, and negative charges are on the ground, and as soon as a tree or a church steeple closes the gap a little bit, it'll spark it and there'll be a lightning bolt. Well, men and women build charges that way and sometimes you just meet up with somebody who's got your charge. Well that's that electricity wanting to neutralize. You don't have to neutralize it in a flash. You can neutralize it over a period of a few hours and make love so it lasts a long time—two or three hours maybe. Actually if you're pretty compassionate it doesn't have to be that long. You can get to where you can get tantric pretty fast with somebody who knows how to do it with you.

*Q: Da Vinci said, "I come to this world very rarely."*

Kind of a spacey thing to say, isn't it? We cycle with the God stuff eternally and every so often it comes through in interesting-shaped lumps and stuff. Normal bell curve of distribution of lumps of God stuff.

*Q: [unintelligible] …* You have to work all the time. And you can take as much responsibility as you want. Anybody can be as heavy as he wants to be. All you've got to do is just accept the workload and start polishing that one and you'll get more workload. And you just keep on truckin'.

*Q: … Who is they?*

Us.

*Q: … You mean we pile more workload on each other?*

On ourselves. I are we in corporate agreement. We are I, I are we.

It feels very stoned. I was just going to say that we should cut it loose right now. Perfect timing. Alrighty. I was really happy to get to come to Goddard, and I really got my head massaged. I feel like we really did bump heads and get in there and communicate some and that's really a groove because something happened. We're going next to Rhode Island.

God Bless you all and thank you for having us here.

*Getting into Burlingame State Park in Rhode Island was a bit of a myste-rious trip. You have to imagine what it'd be like for a gang of hippies going around trying to get directions. And everybody we'd ask said, "Oh you want to go to Burlingame State Park, you've got to see Mr. Ego." "Mr. Ego? What? Are these people putting us on? Mr. Ego, what are they doing to us about this? MR. EGO?" Finally, after a bunch of messing around, we found the office of Mr. John C. Rego, and we figured that one out.*

SUNDAY MORNING SERVICE
BURLINGAME STATE PARK, RHODE ISLAND
29 NOVEMBER 1970

We ought to do a Sunday Morning Service every Sunday morning. I found that I was kind of a chicken this morning from not being out in the cold grey dawn often enough. It felt like this was Thanksgiving morning a lot. It's Thanksgiving country; it's where they started it. This is the first time we've had a chance to stop and give thanks that we could do this at all, that we could come out and be safe across the country.

According to the bets, you couldn't go out there in the middle of the country like us and make it. All we had to do was go out and talk to folks face to face and be real with them and they'd have to like us. They'd have to love us, because we're not doing anything that any-body shouldn't like us or love us for. It's really been like that. Every-where we've been, everybody we've met has dug us.

I think what I've been learning the most going along here is that there isn't any time when we're not tripping. I've been saying that you don't ever come down. You just have a different trip now and then for a while. But I've been finding out more and more as you go along that every little thing that you do and think and be in your head matters in the overall system. And if way back inside your head you're not being on top of it, then something you're going to run into from out there is going to be a reflection of that.

I was talking to somebody who was back in that old trip again about how we only use ten percent of our brain and that when science finds out how to help us use the other ninety percent of our brain we'll be really smart. I told him I was already in touch with the other ninety per cent of my brain and that I called it my Higher Self and that it was the same phenomenon that Jesus referred to when he spoke of "my Father which art in Heaven." It's the rest of our head.

It works like this: If you don't get in touch with your Higher Self, then you can have one man's finite material-plane intelligence to use. The only way you can get in touch with your Higher Self is to not offend it, because if you offend it in any way it won't have anything to do with you. It's pure, and you've got to be as pure as it is.

And where we here are time bound, your Higher Self is eternal and is in eternity, which is to say a non-space/time place. You can know that you have another self that's a part of this self, that you can communicate with, that's eternal, and that this one is going to molder up and you'll eventually get done with it sooner or later and it'll fall apart like an old school bus. But there's another part that doesn't do that because it doesn't have to follow the laws of time and space like rot and entropy.

If you be in too much of a hurry you run out from under your Higher Self, and if you don't try hard enough you don't connect with it. But if you have real courage, and if you really move on out behind it, you can connect so that when you move, you move with the strength of the universe. If you're swimming across the Mississippi, it's you and the Mississippi, but if you're swimming with it, you are the Mississippi. It's that way with your Higher Self.

If you don't come into contact with it you're just one more tripper here on the planet, using up a certain amount of oxygen, needing a certain amount of square-foot ground to bury your crap in. Now, people have known about the Higher Self and how to be in touch with it for thousands and thousands of years. It used to be that we were never out of touch with it. I think we were in touch with it all the time, and I think what they call the fall of man is getting loose from being in touch with it.

We talk about the Golden Mean—that if you're unintegrated in your personality, if you're not in contact with your Higher Self, then everything you're trying to do, you're also doing the opposite at the same time. If you're not integrated you can't do anything, because anything you do, the opposite will also happen to the same extent—the laws of action and reaction that take place are part of the material plane.

But if you're straight with your Higher Self, everything that you try to do is backed up by the power of the universe, and you can make real change happen. You can make change happen that doesn't change back. You can make change happen that's not just apparent change.

Now it's fairly easy to get to where you're integrated—like any time that you and your old lady have got off well and you came off at the same time and you dropped it to her and she dropped it to you and you split your energy, you're pure right there and you're in touch with your Higher Self and anything you do right then is perfect.

But if you forget and fall back into your old habits and forget that you were in a perfect place and that you were a perfect being, you slide back out of it again, so a lot of the teachings are just about how to not forget that you're a perfect being, because if you forget it you make mistakes, if you don't forget it you don't make mistakes.

If you can say that there's something in me that is identical with all that, and by *identical* mean that it is the same, and don't ever forget that, you can stay plugged into that. And if you forget and say, "I'm weak and evil and ain't cool, I'm afraid," like that, you pull your plug and cut loose from your energy—and then you'll just be slipping your clutch. That's what it's like when you lose it with your Higher Self— you keep trying, you keep pushing, you keep struggling, but nothing happens. You wonder, "Wow, man, where did I get unconnected?"

I was talking yesterday about policy levels about psychedelics, and I've been thinking more about it, and I've got more information about it. I've had to cop to psychedelics because they taught me where my Higher Self was—that I had one. I can find it now with or without.

We've come all the way across the country and we've made it this far and we've got a good look at what's going on. I've had a chance to get to talk to folks—like it was really good to get to talk with the camper fellow who came on in an article in the paper about, "We've been trying to keep the hippies out of Burlingame for years and here someone comes and invites them in for free. Where's that at?" I got to talk to that fellow and tell him where it was at about the way we use psychedelics for spiritual things, and we talked it over and I found myself agreeing with him on funny places.

He said, "There's a bunch of thirteen-year-old kids out there. See 'em? Would you tell them to take LSD?"

I said, "No."

He said "Huh?"

I said, "No."

He said, "Why not?"

I said, "It's too strong. Not wrong, just strong. Really strong."

Well, I think LSD really did a thing, but I don't think it's got as much juice in it as it used to have.

I've been gaining compassion with the cops in this journey across the country because I never talked with so many before. I begin to see that the majority of them are peace officers, that they're interested in keeping the peace, that they don't want people to hurt other people, that if a whole bunch of people can be together and someone comes in drunk and starts busting them up, their job is to come get the fellow that's busting them up and let the other folks do their thing. That's really what most of them are about. And I got a look at us through their eyes from that.

It was difficult to explain to them about why somebody would jump through a front window of Blum's, you know, that kind of thing. Some dude did that in San Francisco—Blum's is a candy shop, cake and pastries and stuff—and some dude on acid jumped through the front window of it. Now it's very hard to get somebody to say that that kind of behavior is not weird. They say, "Yeah, it looks weird to me, man, right through the front window." And I understand why they call acid a dangerous drug, because it looks scary to them.

Well I really think that psychedelics are going to help get this country different. Psychedelics have already got this country different a lot. I think I can make folks understand about organics, and I'm willing to go ahead being a psychedelic-type teacher on the basis of doing it with organics … what grows in the woods, as the camper man said to me yesterday. But I am not willing to do that for acid, because it's got too funny a name; too many weird people have done too many weird things on it. If I'm talking to anybody about acid, I'd like to be able to say that we aren't taking acid, and have it be the truth.

INA MAY: *My first chance to learn anything about midwifery from someone who had actually been trained in obstetrics (or midwifery) happened during our few days' stopover in Burlingame Park in Rhode Island. A local obstetrician knocked on our bus door, explained that he had read a newspaper report about the three babies who had already been born on the Caravan, and asked if I would like some midwifery training.*

*Of course I would. I quickly invited over Pamela and Margaret (my friends who had helped me with the three births), and we spent the next few hours drinking tea and learning from Dr. Louis LaPere—sterile technique, how to measure blood pressure, how to perform infant cardiopulmonary resuscitation, how to deal with an umbilical cord wrapped around a baby's neck at birth, how to stop a hemorrhage, how to draw and safely administer an injection, and how to administer the various tests that are necessary for pregnant women. He gave us prenatal vitamins, a copy of the handbook that most U.S. obstetricians used at that time, a blood pressure cuff, a box of sterile gloves, various scissors and clamps, syringes, prenatal vitamins, and medications to be used in the event of hemorrhage.*

*The next birth took place near Nashville—again, at a park. The baby, his mother's first, had the cord tightly wrapped three times around his neck. Thanks to Louis's clear teaching, I was able to deal with this situation and to learn early in my career that such babies can be born without injury.*

*The second problem at this birth was that this same baby was unable to breathe on his own. Again, because of Louis's seminar, I positioned the baby and gave him a breath. To my relief and joy, he took a deep breath, turned from gray-blue to a rosy pink, and yelled with great strength. What a thrilling moment this was for me, for the baby's parents, and for everyone present! Every time I see this young man (who now has two children of his own), I remember that moment.*

UNIVERSITY OF RHODE ISLAND
KINGSTON, RHODE ISLAND
3 DECEMBER 1970

*Q: The question in my mind is, okay, you have it in written form but, you know, the religion is much more than the laws, it's a whole culture. Can intellectual processes capture that?*

You don't do it through intellectual processes. What you do is you telepathically tap into the one great world religion, which is only one, which has no name, and all of the other religions are merely maps of that.

BROWN UNIVERSITY
PROVIDENCE, RHODE ISLAND
4 DECEMBER 1970

This is the first time that I've ever been in the state of Rhode Island, but it's not the first time I've been in this state. Now people have been coming on to me for the last ten days and saying, "What did you come to Rhode Island for?" I guess we came to Rhode Island just to tell you that love is real and that how you be makes a difference in how it is for everybody.

On the way to our next gig, the Caravan passed through the town of Ripley, New York. We arrived in this small town and found out that one of the ladies on one of the buses was going into labor. It turned out that because of where the parking places were, our bus was right in front of the church, and we stretched down the street for blocks and blocks and blocks. The birthing was a good birthing; Mary was into what she was doing, and she did a pretty good job. For Ina May, it was one of her first birthings where she was actually the midwife in charge. And the town was very sweet to us while we were refilling our tanks and refrigerators and everything in the stores up and down the street. We'd used the phone in the church a couple of times and they knew we were having a baby, so when the baby arrived we went to the church and told them the baby arrived—and they rang the church bells so everybody in Ripley would know that we had our baby as we came through there.

*When we got to New York City, we parked the buses on diagonal parking meters all around Washington Square. We were an amazing thing.*

It feels like to me the realest thing we can do right now is pay attention to where we be, and to what it's really like. When you're driving into New York City it starts being New York City somewhere back in the middle of Connecticut ... it feels like. And we been driving all that way on concrete, past all that concrete and all those buildings ... and we come to Union Square here. It's got a few trees and a little bit of grass, and the remainder of the wildlife, which is the birds and the rats.

Somebody pointed out when I got here that the dark bumps out in the white snow were rats. And at first I thought, with that kind of American sterilize-it-all sort of uptightness place, I thought, "Rats? What kind of a city is this?" And now I see that if it wasn't for the rats and the birds I don't know who'd be carrying the mail, because the rats are life, trying to make it in this little park. The birds are life trying to make it here. And these trees are life, and they're all making it. They've been laying down concrete here for a couple of hundred years, and the life is still making it.

Now there's the rats and the birds and us. And we're life, still making it. Getting here and being here is just as miraculous as if we'd come around the Horn in a clipper ship, or if we came across the Atlantic in those leaky old boats that Columbus came in.

There's a few folks here from New York, I see. Now folks that came with me know what we're doing, we've been doing it for a long time. And we should make some contact with folks that live here, which is an important thing to do ... Let's just have sort of immediate questions from folks who walked by and saw this and said, "What you all doing?" [Silence.]

Well if everybody's got all that covered, I think where we're at is that it's okay for us to be around here on the streets for a while, so we better have us a good breakfast. You can replace sleep with food sometimes. We're going to go out onto Long Island and find ourselves a place to hang out for a while. We'll go on out of the city like we came in, we'll just caravan on out.

There's folks in other buses parked in other places than here, is that right? Okay, let's figure everybody get all their buses over here and assembled in this parking lot at nine o'clock, and when everybody's assembled here at nine o'clock, then we'll truck on out. This is like touching second base. Now we're going back toward the home plate.

God Bless you all, thank you for getting up early in the morning. Let's go have breakfast.

*There were several towns—one south of San Francisco, and Goddard College, and Stony Brook out on Long Island—where we picked up new people that joined up with us. And that was one of the ways how we grew, from a Caravan of twenty-five buses to fifty full-size school buses and a host of other smaller equipment, including the now-infamous Cadillac camper, which was a big old Cadillac with a big old camper on it—it was pretty fast and pretty big.*

STATE UNIVERSITY OF NEW YORK AT STONY BROOK
LONG ISLAND, NEW YORK
8 DECEMBER 1970

Possibly everybody here might not be familiar with the OM. It's just your simplest, purest note, the one that you can put out with all your juice behind it because you know it's your solid note and you're not going to lose it or blow it or it's not going to crack on you or anything. And if everybody does that, that's what makes the real perfect one is everybody doing their OM real strong.

We've been out on the road six or seven weeks in this Caravan, but in a way we've been out on the road for a longer time than that. I've been having meetings in San Francisco for about five years now. And we started off not knowing much, but knowing that there was something besides the material-plane meat part of existence. When we first got the class together we were like a research instrument, and we read everything we could on religion, magic, superstition, ecology, extrasensory perception, fairy tales, collective unconscious, folkways, and math and physics. And we began finding things out as we went along about the nature of the mind.

We found out that people are telepathic a lot of the time, even when they may not think they are. We read various kinds of books on the subject—Italian researchers using LSD for telepathy experiments in 1958. They discontinued the experiments because they said they couldn't get enough telepathy happening because they said the hallucinations started interfering too much. They wanted to have the kind of words-ring-in-the-head telepathy and they weren't satisfied with television.

And as we kept on studying that and finding out what was that about, we said there's probably got to be some kind of a best system that you can run this kind of a thing on that works good for everybody, because immediately certain kinds of things come to mind.

What if somebody comes and looks in your head and you're not ready for them to. Suppose you didn't make up the bed and the dishes are dirty. What does it feel like if you've got something in your head that you're afraid somebody's going to find out about. How do you be with people when you all share the same head. What about a political science for a territory with no boundaries, non-space/time. We also saw that it was not that some people could get other people's heads, it was that some people couldn't hardly help getting other people's heads, considering their various states of sanity.

And we used to, way back, think of ourselves like the George Washingtons and the Thomas Jeffersons of the telepathic plane who were going to hammer out a Constitution. We started putting this thing together, and then it started getting recognizable as the pieces fell in. And we saw that it looked just like Christianity, and it looked just like Buddhism, and it looked just like every religion, because that's what a religion is.

Actually religion is re-legion: people coming together again. That's how I got to be a teacher; in the process of working out what we worked out, I got to a place where I'd give advice on how to trip, and then I found out life was a trip. Then I had to give advice on how to live.

*Q: What are the things you believe in? Yourself?*

I believe in myself, but I believe in the totality of the universe.

*Q: ... A supernatural God?*

God may be super and God may be natural, but not supernatural.

*Q: I didn't understand what you meant by that ...*

What I meant by that was that God is us and the building and the grass and the trees, the total All of everything. And as to what I meant in what I said to him about the idea of supernatural, there isn't anything supernatural. Everything is natural. So you can't say that some is supernatural. Now there are other planes that are visible to us, if we prepare ourselves properly. But you don't need to go to those places looking for God, because God is right here and now all the time, wherever you are. Not supernatural, not some place else but just right here. Okay?

*Q: ... Yeah. Another question: Why do you believe in God?*

Why. Well, under my definition, God is the total All. And it's silly not to believe in that because it's self-evident.

*Q: ... Why do you call it a god?*

That's the name by which it's known. See, people ask a question that goes like, "What is God?" But that's a problem in set theory, because God is the prime set that contains everything else, so you can't say, "What is God?" If you have a question that says, "What is the absolute totality of everything?" the answer is, "God." So it's an answer rather than a question.

*Q: How do you assess the relationship between what you say and believe in and what's on the blackboard behind you?*

Which part? Genetics thing? Right. I don't find that to be any contradiction or anything. I see the dance of the genes and the dance of the minds as the dance of the universe. Like the Scopes trial was a long time ago. I call people monkeys a lot, because they look like monkeys to me. You know, it's just self-evident.

I ran across that in the Declaration of Independence the other day, and it really blew my mind. Those cats really had soul. They started off, and they didn't quibble, they didn't give any footnotes, they didn't say who said so, but they said, "We hold these truths to be self-evident." Isn't that neat?

*Q: They couldn't say anything else.*

Wow. I'm hip. It's really beautiful. But it's been such a long time since we've had people around who would say, "It's self-evident." Amen. I like that.

*Q: I'm interested in out-of-body states. I was wondering what experience you've had.*

I've had a few experiences coming out of a dream into out-of-body states. I think the most striking one I had was when I heard the baby complaining, sounding rather alarmed in the middle of the night, and I went to her bedside to see what was happening, and when I got there I tried to do something and found I had forgotten my bod, left it back in the bedroom. She really wanted me to see her and I couldn't. I felt I couldn't do anything from where I was, so I went back to the bedroom and there was my bod on the bed. I got inside my bod and then I could sort of roll over and I could face the bed or face the ceiling or whatever without turning my physical bod over, but I couldn't wake it up right away.

I went kind of exploring in through there and I found I could move a foot. So I started shaking that foot real hard. I shook my foot so hard that it finally woke up my conscious mind too, and I made the transition from the dream state into the conscious state without loss of consciousness. I came out with me, got back up and went into the bedroom where the baby was and looked at her, and when I looked at her she didn't cop that I was there at first but she started wiggling her hand real hard. She wiggled her hand until she woke up and I picked her up. She was having some kind of a trip, and when she could split fields with me it cooled her out. I put her back to bed and then I took my bod back to bed, too.

But it was really that definite—that sensation of mobile center of consciousness. I don't seek that kind of stuff a great deal because I think what you do is seek for enlightenment—the highest you can get—and then you get into more access to that kind of stuff as you go along. But if you hang up on the phenomena, it may bar you from getting higher.

*Q: Do you think that mankind collectively has a goal or a purpose?*

The purpose is tripping, not where you're tripping to. And mankind is here on the planet to groove—that's our purpose. We have this universe for us to come here and groove in with all of this fantastic grooving equipment that we have. We've got eyeballs and ears, touch, and so on, and then we've got a whole set of telepathic senses for all the material-plane senses.

We're supposed to get out and interact with the universe and groove. Now the thing that gets mankind in trouble a lot is future-tripping. Like I think the communists blew it when they said it's all right for us to wipe out this generation for the sake of the next one. No, man, you got to be cool with this one right now, because the trip is here and now, all the time, and if you sell out your here and now for the future you have no value in the here and now and none in the future either.

[*Q: unintelligible*]   Non-linear and linear. Okay. One two three four five six seven eight nine ten is linear, and non-linear is all at once. You can use *gestalt* for *non-linear* if you like, that's a good word. Gestalt means the idea that the whole is more than the sum of its parts. On a linear system the whole is equal to the sum of its parts. The way in which you learn how to do some things is in a linear fashion, but the way that you recognize faces is completely non-linear.

Everybody has a different face and you can tell them all apart and you can sort out millions of them and make a flash on each one. That's a non-linear mind function—the system by which you sort all those faces—and it's fantastic. They're all about nine inches high and about six inches wide, and you've got a limited number of colors and shapes and positions and a limited amount of space to put it in, and your mind can flash each one, separate, and you can not only see family resemblances but you can see little threads like that that run out through thousands and thousands of people with that gestalt pattern-recognition kind of consciousness.

But on a linear thing you have somebody like Professor Bertillon, who had a system for catching criminals by measuring their nose so many centimeters, their ears so many centimeters, and you have a system of numbers by which you can recognize somebody. That's a linear way to do it. A digital computer doesn't even multiply; it only counts real fast. And an analog computer is like your gas gauge and it says, this varies as that varies, and so your gas gauge is a non-linear kind of computer. The kind of gauge that the gas comes out of the pump into the car with is a linear computer, as a line of stuff goes through something that turns around and measures it. Those are different kinds of linear and non-linear functions. The heaviest stuff you do is mostly non-linear.

*Q: Do you think that our technology and our spirituality are creating one another and will eventually move towards a unity?*

I think our technology right now is like an extended speed trip that mankind has been on for a couple of hundred years. The industrial revolution was just like methedrine in the arm of mankind.

Aldous Huxley said there had been only one new sin invented since the original seven deadly, and it was speed. And conceptual speed, mechanical speed, chemical speed, electronic speed, and all those kinds of speed are all the same thing.

*Q: What direction do you think mankind is moving in?*

I think that mankind has moved into a superficial satisfying of his desire for sensory stuff. I think that we satisfy our senses a whole lot with technology: We have rock and roll if you're into ear and movies if you're into eye and motorcycles if you're into bod. I know many people who are so surrounded by their electric titillators that they have no idea what life is really about. And folks who are plugged on to a rock and roll set of earphones or some kind of technological trip like that are lost souls, man, because they aren't going to find out where it's at.

I think we've got to learn to give up the junk. We've got to scrap the tinker-toy set, because it's really overrated. I think what we're going to do is we're going to quit gratifying the gross material senses so much, because it costs so much for all of mankind to gratify those senses, and we're going to start learning to gratify our finer senses, which are spiritual, and there's enough spiritual stuff to go around all the time. So the direction is for us to go simpler and simpler with material, and you can get pretty fancy out in there if you be simple with material.

*Q: Well, what form do you think our technology will take, because certainly you can't deny the fact that our technology continually accelerates.*

Well, I think we have to deny that our technology continually accelerates or … A friend of mine had a 650 Triumph and he was trying to fix the throttle cable, so he had the throttle cable off and he had the motor started and he knocked it off the stand and it fell over on its side and it kicked the throttle wide open and it just screamed for a few seconds and then exploded. And that's what this culture will do if somebody doesn't turn off the key. This depression that's happening right now is the culture collectively turning off the key, saying, "No, man, you can't drive that fast if I'm going to ride with you. Somebody's going to have to slow this car down, man, it's getting dangerous … too fast, too leaky to go so fast."

Q: … Do you think it's possible to do that?

Yes, I think that mankind has got to back off this speed trip if he intends to survive on the planet.

Q: … Do you think that on the other hand technology could be the very medium by which we do survive on the planet?

As soon as it starts becoming compassionately applied for the sake of all people, instead of un-compassionately for the sake of corporations, which are soulless entities that have growth drives and no intelligence or soul. Technology isn't going to lead us to any kind of enlightenment. If we're lucky we'll get loose from technology enough to get enlightened. The major bar to enlightenment for the people of this culture is their technology.

Q: … You were talking about non-linear reality, and it appears to me that the world in general is moving toward nonlinear reality and our technology is taking us there.

No, I'm specifically trying to disabuse you of the notion that the technology is what is saving you, because the technology isn't saving you. I feel like sometimes the universe is going on and somebody's saying, "Turn off the machine," and somebody's saying, "I can't hear you for the machine."

Q: I'd like to get onto a different track. It's actually a problem that my husband and I have run into. First of all, we went to San Francisco to see you and when we came back we … you know, in San Francisco people know what you're about. They know about you. And we came back and we wanted to turn some friends on, and trying to explain what you're about is very difficult, you know? You can say, well, you're into a spiritual … well, you're into a truth type thing. And I would like you to review or perhaps explain to me in a condensed form … like I know what it is, but how to express what it is….

What we're doing? We're a group of folks who discovered that you don't have to get a fire but that you can make a fire. And so we're making a fire. And once you get far enough into making a fire, then you find out that that's the way all fires happened—they got made. And then you know as much about fire making as anybody knows. And so we're just into fire making.

*[Stephen:] I had almost forgotten this next part of the Stonybrook gig. When Alan Graf reminded me about it, I asked him to tell what he remembered about that gig. I thought of the title myself: "**The Donnybrook at Stonybrook**."*

ALAN GRAF: *Around 1969–70 I was a student at the University of Stonybrook. I had been involved with Students for a Democratic Society (SDS) but had become disillusioned with the group due to the amount of rhetoric and infighting that took place on a regular basis.*

*One afternoon I was sitting in my dormitory room on campus after having taken a strong dose of "orange sunshine." I was laying down on my bed looking at the walls moving when two hippies came into the common area in the dormitory. They said they were from "the Caravan" and spoke with each other in a language of terms that I had never heard before. They were incredibly interesting, and from their conversations about the "energy of the moment" they gathered a crowd of students around them.*

*They then started talking to each other about how one of them "had a stash with the other." They proceeded to speak with each other in public about some of the most personal stuff I had ever heard anyone talk about. One of them admitted that they got angry when the other one "hogged the juice." All this conversation caught my attention and wrenched it away from the moving walls.*

*I followed these folks from the dorm to their Caravan and met many hippies who had traveled from San Francisco across the country to talk about peace and how peace and love were the essential ingredients to changing the world. They invited me to hear their teacher Stephen speak that night at the local meeting hall.*

I went down to the meeting hall and saw a bunch of the hippies gathered on stage. Stephen lifted a ram's horn to his mouth and blew a clear note, which sort of tuned the meeting up. He then spoke to the crowd about how the Caravan got to Stonybrook and about the message he was trying to talk about across the country.

At one point, some of my old colleagues from SDS started to heckle him. They said that "peace was bullshit" and that without violence and confrontation we would "lose to the man." Stephen at first tried to reason with them, but at one point they demanded that he give up leading the meeting. So he acquiesced and said, "Okay, it's your meeting, I will sit back and listen." He sat back and didn't say anything, and the SDS guys tried to take it over.

Within minutes, the meeting turned from a real focused spiritual meeting to one of chaos. People were shouting at each other, and the vibes just got worse and worse. Then, some folks stood up and said, "Hey Stephen, how about taking back the meeting?"

Stephen got up and asked the crowd in a respectful way if they wanted him back, and the majority of the crowd yelled, "Yeah!"

After that, I remember Stephen talking about how the Caravan was looking for a home and that if they ever found one that got too crowded they would start other places where they could practice their beliefs.

I left that meeting thinking that I had met "my people" and that I would eventually join the Caravan and practice their way of life.

I lived on the Farm (the home the Caravan found) from 1972 to 1984, left to go to law school to become a lawyer, fought the good fight, and then returned in 2006 to the hippie Mecca homeland, The Farm, in Summertown, Tennessee.

*I was scheduled to speak in the Princeton Chapel, but when I got there I was astonished because the Princeton Chapel is a pretty good-sized Gothic cathedral—the fanciest place that I'd ever talked.*

PRINCETON UNIVERSITY CHAPEL
PRINCETON, NEW JERSEY
12 DECEMBER 1970

I think I ought to start with talking about attention. In the same way that when Einstein said $E = mc^2$, with that same is-ness of identity, attention is energy. And nothing ever prospers without a lot of attention.

Now, the founding fathers who started this country, I feel, were spiritual people in some ways, but in some ways they were materialists. Now, this country has put its attention into getting material things, because it was based on the idea, in the very beginning, that there was all this limitless wilderness out there. And if anybody didn't get along with you, just push them out to the edge of town. That's how the United States grew across the continent is the people who couldn't get along with anybody else just moved out to the edge of town.

And we come on as a country very big on the material plane. Somebody said it took the gross national product of Egypt twenty years to build the Great Pyramid. If we put the gross national product of the United States behind something for twenty years we could put the Great Pyramid in orbit. Very heavy in the material plane.

When I was in school I heard about the great debates that had gone on, and nobody had ever told me that people knew the answers to any of those questions. I just heard there were great debates … like church and state, that that was debated. Nobody could know. When they started the country, the idea of separation of church and state was so that the church could exist without being hassled by the state and vice versa. That was the function of it.

The money didn't always say, "In God we trust." That was put on not by the founders but by the Republicans under Eisenhower.

So we look back at men like George Washington, and they look so awesome big, you know. They really took a lot on their own karma. Consider what kind of a mind or where your head had to be at to start off something like, "We hold these truths to be self-evident." Isn't that far out? You ever hear of anybody so heavy as to say anything like that since then? And the founding fathers of the country tried to, through the way they wrote the Constitution and all that—Declaration of Independence, things about life, liberty, and the pursuit of happiness, all that—tried to make the material plane be the way the real Church is. And this country didn't live up to that, because the country was also founded in violence.

*Q: Could we say that television is a de facto church, since it's now the de facto government?*

If so, it's a funny kind of a church, because what it does is it calls you to satisfying your material-plane senses. It tries to sucker you into smell and into taste, and eat this, and smell this, and ride this, and put this in your nose.

Now, a materialistic culture grows on people experiencing something. So you experience all the things in your natural environment, and then somebody makes you up something else to experience and you experience that. "Dig this, I just made it." And after you experience a thing, you've got to store it somewhere. After you listen to your records for a while, you've got to stash your records. After you look at your paintings, you've got to have a place to put your paintings. You get into a thing-storage problem.

You get into who's got the neatest thing. I read in the paper today that a Velasquez painting outsold as the highest-priced painting of all time one of Rembrandt's. Somebody in heavy competition about what they're going to experience with their eyes. That's pretty heavy, isn't it?

It works out that finally you cannot be satisfied on the material plane ... due as much to problems in shipping and handling, I suppose, as anything else, because the material plane takes part in the first three laws of thermodynamics: You can't win on it; you can't break even on it; you lose a little bit on it. That's the material plane. It would be a grim-sounding universe without Spirit. The material plane with Spirit is Heaven and without Spirit is hell. And Spirit can only manifest itself on the material plane through the agency of compassionate human beings who will make themselves a reservoir for it.

*Q: Would you talk about lifestyle?*

Yes. That's an important place. It seems like the cheapest stuff you can eat is the stuff that's good for you. So a piece of you ought to be concerned with diet. Getting the world together has got to include dietary reform, and it means we're going to have to get into inexpensive stuff that doesn't have to be manufactured a lot, because lots of manufacturing costs lots of money. And you don't eat meat because if everybody eats meat, there's not enough food for everybody. But if everybody doesn't eat meat, there's enough food for everybody.

I think we're meant for a vegetarian diet actually. My body works better on it. We've been into a lot of soybeans; soybeans are good for protein. And I don't do much dairy products because I feel that's just part of the meat system on another level. I don't do chicken or fish because they're just like cows except they live in different places. So, all in all, you can make it on fruits and vegetables and grains and beans and all that kind of stuff and you can live really well.

*Q: Do you think that eating meat cuts down on your psychic powers?*

I've been to animal killings and I've been to rice boilings and rice boilings have better vibes.

*Q: What is the cause for doubt about experiencing God, like where they say, "Well I've got to be able to see the thing."*

One of the things that causes the doubt currently is the temptation of the entire super-rich material-plane nature of the culture to pull you away from the idea that there's anything important about mind and about learning to get yourself together and about making changes in yourself instead of in somebody else at gunpoint.

Here's why when you tell somebody they're a materialist they don't like it: When you tell somebody they're a materialist you're telling them, "You're strung out on things, man. You're strung out, you know, addicted." That's what you tell somebody when you tell them they're a materialist. Nobody's ego likes being told they're strung out. That's the last thing anybody wants to hear, and their ego will tend to defend the idea that they aren't strung out, as much as possible. But being hooked on the material plane is about the worst addiction you can get into, because it can make it so that you don't notice that there's anything else.

*Q: I'd like to know more about telepathy …*

The thing about being telepathic is that you can't be too conservative about what you think is telepathy. It doesn't mean just the telephone in the head—"Hello, Dr. Watson, are you there?"—kind of thing. It's not just that, but it's a whole complex of things, like the sense of presence in your whole bod is one. Everybody just knows that you inhabit your whole bod. A lot of you probably got your tail turned off because you've been sitting in the pews. Notice and see it's still there. Feel that improvement in the body vibration? That feels a lot easier to me right now because folks were reminded to pay attention that their body was cool. That's a level of it.

It's also that we have these seven energy centers. Well actually we have a lot more than that, but we have the seven ones they talk about in yoga; like your anal center, sexual center, solar plexus, heart chakra, throat chakra, third eye, and crown chakra are the seven major energy centers ... the bottom one being the root support which is that large piece of muscle just between your rectum and whatever lies north of that, depending on your sex.

And the next one is actually your sexual equipment, some of the glandular equipment for that. Now a chakra, that's just Sanskrit for wheel, and it works like an eye iris, or like a sea anemone. You know how a sea anemone just opens and opens and then something disturbs it and it closes again. Your chakras are like that. And so you're always trying to open them all. You want them to all be open because you're having telepathy between each set because of resonances.

If you pluck the E string on one guitar, the E string on another guitar will resonate with it, and if you pluck the G string, the G string will resonate with it. Right now I'm resonating my throat chakra a lot by talking loud. Singing does that, too. A violin is a throat-amplifier. You make a material-plane noise out there, but the vibe you put into it is your throat chakra. That's why violin music is so schmaltzy.

When your sexual chakra comes on, you know what that feels like. You know what it feels like when you get the electric signal when it gets time to take a crap. There's a certain kind of opening electricity there. That's the opening of that chakra. Now this stomach chakra here, the telepathy that's transmitted on the wave-band of this chakra from people to people is either confidence or paranoia. If this chakra is open, well, that makes a lot of confidence happen. If it's clenched, that makes paranoia.

Your heart chakra ... sometimes you may feel an emotional thing, real heavy kind of throb. That's how I sense it when I feel it a lot. Throat chakra ... noise. You ought to be able to holler just as loud as you can holler. Third eye ... this vision looks pretty good to me right now. It should look that way to you now. Look pretty psychedelic to you right now? That's third eye functioning. Third eye's psychedelic vision. They call it divine vision.

And then the crown chakra … Now when they used to talk about the divine right of kings, that was before separation of church and state, and that meant that a king was supposed to have a crown chakra which was open. And the material-plane crown was a representation of the fact that his crown chakra was supposed to be open. Now your crown chakra being open, that's your brain. And if your brain isn't clenched, you ought to be smart.

*Q: Does tantric yoga mean bisexuality?*

I never heard of such a thing, myself. It seems so formal. I don't think that any of us should be too proud to vibe with one another. I know we've been taught that it's not very cool to touch each other very much, but it really is cool to touch each other. It's a fine means of communication.

I talked to a lady in Rhode Island who was ninety-three years old, and when I held her hand we were in close communication. At one point I moved around and I put my knee up against her knee like I would one of my hippy lady friends and pushed against her knee. And she either had to push back or be moved over a little ways, and so she pushed back.

We didn't quibble or anything, and she didn't say anything. She was ninety-three years old and wanted to exchange some juice. She wanted to feel somebody feel her non-conceptually.

It was like that with the man who was in charge of the park who shook my hand. And he was telling us that he had been in that park in Rhode Island since the trees had been planted and that he dug us better than anybody that had been there since. And while he was telling us that, he quit shaking my hand and let it sit still and kind of let the vibes settle.

And pretty soon he was just standing there talking, holding my hand. He held my hand a long time, and he felt good, because he was in his hand and it was warm and alive and right there. Then we let go, and he never said anything about that. We didn't say anything on the material plane; we didn't say anything with words about that. We didn't have to, because touch is a means of communication, too. And you can get telepathic on any means of communication; that's what's neat about communication.

To get telepathic on touch is called tantric yoga, and it's the yoga of making love, spiritually if you will, and it's just simply opening up all your things. I said something about the seven major centers; there's also centers in the shoulder joints, and the hip joints, and then more specifically both eyes, and in the nose. There's a whole class of human behavior that comes from a clenched nose chakra, and if you've got conservative nose it makes you act in certain ways. People are determined by being hung up in a sense. If you're way out into eye, people can move you around with eye stuff, if you're hung up in ear, people can magic you around with ear stuff.

The only way you can keep from getting magicked around is to have all your senses balanced and be coming on with all of them at once all the time. Considerable amount of juice.

*Q: What causes the rushes?*

That's *kundalini*. For a long time I read all the books in Sanskrit and whatnot, trying to find out about kundalini, but when I finally found out what it was … it's just that current of life force that flows up your body. If you have a lot of it, it makes you be like a crisp lettuce leaf, and if you haven't got much of it, it makes you be like a limp lettuce leaf. And it's that thing, the one that makes you erect and alert. If it's not flowing you sort of collapse, and if it's flowing a whole lot you're stoned. So that's just that energy flowing up. Any time we come to a heavy agreement or understanding, it increases the energy level all over.

*Q: Could you talk about Deity?*

I look at Deity through the idea of gestalt. Each one of us is a creator, and each one of us is creating our own universe as it comes in on us.

Each one of us has an aura, which is that field of electrical vibration that surrounds us. And if you talk about one person having an aura like that, then if everyone has an aura like that you have to say that there is a resultant field that is everybody's whole thing. The idea of gestalt is that the whole is more than the sum of its parts, not the same as. And that the sum of us is more than us. That's the way I get to that kind of Deity.

In Sanskrit they break it up into functions, and they have different gods and things talking about different functions. I don't do that so much, but Deity functioning through the laws of physics—something falls thirty-two feet per second per second on earth—is Deity just as much or exactly the same or even more than a concept of Deity as an outside entity. The resultant thing is us. It is not outside. We are part of the All. There is no outside entity.

*Q: God is not outside of us?*

Right. There is no "outside." Being spiritual is maybe like spiritual electro-magnetic ecology, and knowing that we have an ecological niche in the universe. We're not just perched up on the edge of a rock. We're not sitting inside of a spaceship or something. We're part of this trip that's going on. We're part of this thing that's happening. And if we don't recognize that we're part of it, then we relinquish all of our chance for any control of it whatsoever. The idea is that we're supposed to be in control of it. The religious books of all the centuries, and the good-sense tripping instructions of anybody who ever tripped enough to learn how to trip, say that as you sow so you shall reap ... on all the planes.

*[Q: unintelligible]* The question is, she has a need to believe that God is in all of us and in everything, but doesn't know whether that need to believe it is merely a product of wanting to believe it.

Here's the thing, you want someone to guarantee your bet. But it's supposed to be a bet. When you bet on the universe, it's like a bet. You say, "That's the one I say is it, that's where it's at, that's what's going to do it." You don't ask for anything back first. You got to do that first, and that means that you got to come up with the initial energy. It's like priming the pump. You do that and then you don't have to worry about belief anymore, because the universe becomes one with you and you see the universe treat you exactly where you're at, which it does all the time anyway, but you just get to see it better.

*Q: Could you talk a little bit about techniques for realizing one's own spiritual nature?*

Techniques, I don't know. I feel that it's not so much techniques as it is straighten up. Buddha says, "Avoid error." How about that?

*Q: The normal bell curve of distribution can refer to whether people are enlightened, insane, or in between, but will it always be that way?*

He says the normal bell curve of distribution also probably applies to the incidence of enlightenment among the monkeys, and that there's some of them that are enlightened, and some of them that really aren't, and a whole bunch of them that are on the path. And he says, "Will it always be that way?" And the thing is, yes and no, in the sense that there's always a balance between yang and yin, but everybody can be in communion at once. And in communion everybody is enlightened.

*Q: Could you explain to me about ego and ego defenses?*

Nobody consciously wants their ego to defend itself, I don't think. Everybody pays at least some lip service to the idea that you shouldn't be an egomaniac. But people's subconsciouses will do anything. Your subconscious is unscrupulous because it doesn't know what a scruple is. Your subconscious has no value judgments about where it gets its juice. So if you desire anything your subconscious will get it for you.

Now your subconscious is not another room in your head like the basement, it's right there in plain sight. It's right there in front of you all the time, and you don't see it because you choose not to pay attention to it. That's the only reason it's sub.

146

Enlightenment is trying to get people to pay attention to the here and now—to what they're actually doing right now. Now if a person doesn't have much subconscious you should be able to attack their ego and they should be able to laugh. You should be able to climb right up in the middle of their thing and jump on it, and they should be able to say, "So what." And if you can't, it's because they have subconscious.

Now the subconscious has a tendency to cause itself to propagate. It's like a tropism. A flower turns toward the sun because the sun actually makes chemical changes happen along the stem that make it grow and groove in a different way and turn toward the sun. Now that's not a thinking action on that flower's part. And nobody can say that that flower has consciousness, except in its own realm of vegetable. It has vegetable consciousness, but it doesn't turn toward the sun in a self-conscious act. It turns toward the sun because of a tropism.

The flowers that turn toward the sun are called heliotropes. Other flowers, too—sunflowers. Now, the subconscious is only a bundle of tropisms. The consciousness has a fragment of free will, and can actually do something. The bundle of tropisms that the subconscious is will tend to defend itself. It will try to defend itself to exist, but it has no reality.

This is to say that the ego has no reality outside of its existence as the coordinator of a bunch of perceptions. And as anything other than that it doesn't exist. But we have this thing that we call personality.

And your personality is not your ego, your personality is your junk heap of spare parts that you picked up along the line. A lot of people defend their junkyard of spare parts thinking that they're defending themselves.

Having a subconscious is like having a big mean hungry dog. And all you can do for it is not be hungry. If you don't be hungry the dog won't be hungry. So if you can learn to control your own personal desires as you meet them right here in the here and now, your subconscious will no longer be powerful to do anything other than pay attention and be the telepathic communications room.

*Q: Are there any motivations you have?*

Like it says on the front of the bus: "Out to Save the World."

*Q: What is meant by ego death?*

It's deciding that everybody is really smart enough to keep the toilet paper dry without you being there. Sometimes the universe has to chase you around with a stick to get you to cop to that. Ego death is like getting all the rear-view mirrors ripped off your ego so it's just looking out and it's not looking back at itself. It seems to me that you grow ego like barnacles in the material plane … and that you have to be doing something about it all the time, and it can't be a question of ego death and then I'm done with it, because it isn't that way. If you're going to keep on existing in the plane, then you're going to keep having a viewpoint.

And your viewpoint is your ego. So that means you are to pay attention to the rest of the universe, not just yourself. So being worried about not being able to have an ego death is a negative ego trip. But a negative or a positive doesn't make any difference. It is still ego.

*Q: Isn't loving yourself a positive thing?*

Yes, love all things in the universe, not forsaking yourself. You're supposed to love yourself. You're supposed to say, "Wow, man, looky there. Put together clean. Good job by the universe. Look at that opposable thumb work. Rotatable wrists. Pretty fancy. Self-warming." You should put high value into the equipment. You should respect the equipment.

I don't like violent movies that show pictures of folks getting cut up. That causes there to be disrespect for the organism, and makes it look like it's okay to do that, or that it's easy to do that. We have a lot of disrespect for the monkey inherent in our cultural entertainments. I used to hear about these folks in these little religious sects that got a little church out in a farming community somewhere with a funny name, that don't wear lipstick, and they don't smoke cigarettes and all that. I don't either.

The whole material plane and our sensory apparatus together are the bread and butter of our lives. If you're not just stoned by it all the time, you're not paying attention.

*Q: What's your concept of the universe?*

Universe means one turn. By implication it means one truth … means that it's all under one thing, whatever it is. That's about as close as I can get to anything about a concept of the universe. It's all one thing, and here it is.

You don't conceptualize about the universe, you're in it. If you conceptualize about it you get self–other. You've got to be able to identify with the universe. If you've got to identify with the universe, the best thing that you can do is get down home with it. Don't think about it, interact with it. Re-learn leverage for yourself. Don't take leverage on the say-so of some monkey a million years ago. Do your own experiment. Find out yourself about leverage. That's the way to relate with the universe. I don't think being conceptual helps you at all.

*[Q: unintelligible]* We were talking about lifestyle. The buses aren't the lifestyle. The buses are a method of transportation to get us around to do this. We had to soul-search about that before we even left California, about going out in all these buses. Well, one thing about them is we're living pretty cheap. My bus cost $650, and it's home for six people. That's pretty good. It's at a fairly high subsistence level for now.

I don't plan on driving a bus all the time. I can get a lot higher than that if I stop somewhere and park it. Getting into it with the dirt is really where it's at. I'm just coming around here to say, Get into it with the dirt. And as soon as I get done saying that, I'm going to get into it with the dirt.

[Q: unintelligible]   Nobody can consider themselves enlightened or permanently stoned until everybody is. Because nobody can be a Buddha on purpose. You be a Buddha passing through, but as soon as you catch yourself being a Buddha you say, "Bingo, ran it through again, okay, put it back to the beginning," and be a bodhisattva and go back and try to get everybody else off. You don't come into being a Buddha and say, "Okay, take me out of the game, I'm done."

Because if you're a Buddha you're compassionate. And if you're compassionate you say, "Wow, there's other folks that have to be helped out so everybody can make it." So I think there's a natural place that happens when you get stoned that happened to me, where I'd come to a place of being very stoned and then the universe would come on and say, "What do you want from here, right now? You can have anything you want, what do you want?" I'd say, "I want everybody to be stoned. I want everybody to be just like I am right now."

Q: ... Here and now.

Yes, here and now, isn't that neat. Everybody did it, too. Because that was subconscious language. It just doesn't matter if there's quotation marks around it. I just gave a command to everybody's subconscious, and we did it. I just wanted to point that out so we wouldn't lose it.

Q: ... Everything is stoned.

Yes. This is a very here and now thing we have happening right now. We're all here conscious that us monkeys is here doing this trip and that what we put into it—what love, what faith, and what energy—is what makes it be heavy.

*Q: Do you believe that there's a good and an evil?*

I think that there may be a good, but I don't think that there's an evil.
I think there are a multitude of little evils, but I don't think that there
is an evil. I think it's like any center of organization will have a tendency or a tropism toward a little disorganization around the edges of
it to balance it. And that there's positive and negative: The universe is
made out of positive and negative, right down to the finest atom.
There's a positive and a negative piece. It's like the yang and yin:
There's those two little tadpoles, you know, but there's that circle that
surrounds them, and that's the structure, that's the overall of them.
And creation is an overall oneness—not a two-ness at war.

*Q: ... Do you think that people have to distinguish between good and evil?*

Yes. You have to distinguish between good and evil in your life. You
can't ignore what you know about things. I think everybody really
knows where it's at all the time. I think the people who are making
their high wages because of the war trip know it, and are haunted by
it a little bit. I don't think that they can not know that. And I think that
they have to know that to a percentage they're involved in evil.

151

CURTIS HALL
PHILADELPHIA, PENNSYLVANIA
17 DECEMBER 1970

his place we're in right now is a meditative state, and it's strong enough that we can do whatever business we have to do, move around whatever we have to move around. And keep it. We don't have to worry about losing it because we're solid into it. It looks to me like the first thing we have to do is reshuffle the room again. What would it be like if I move back on the stage a ways and a bunch of people move up on the stage? Yeah.

This is a spontaneous meeting of the monkeys, and spontaneous meetings of the monkeys happen in times of great monkey stress. This is a time of extremes, and among those things that are coming on strong is a great spiritual renaissance. I think it's self-evident that mankind is religious and that most people everywhere as soon as they have a chance to settle become religious. I don't expect everyone to know what *religious* is instantly. I didn't myself until fairly recently.

Now if you don't plant a field for a few seasons and you let the field lie, it replenishes and puts energy back into the earth so it can be a fertile field again. This country has lain spiritually fallow for quite a long time, and there's a lot of energy back into the people. People in masses and droves are becoming aware that each person is responsible for their own destiny and that groups of people who make agreements are responsible for their destiny.

This country has so much spiritual energy in it that it's like a super-cooled solution. You can chill water to below freezing and it won't turn solid, it won't turn to ice if it's perfectly pure, but if you add one little piece of dust to it, or one crystal of ice, it'll change to ice instantly.

The country is in that super-cooled state, as such, maybe spiritually in season like a mare is in season, and there are a lot of folks trying to make that contact with all those people, to unify that thing. Now what's happening in this country is outrageous. The television has closed up communication so tight that it's direct cause and effect. A ten-year-old can understand that the Secretary of Defense says it's awful hard for him to save any more lives and keep the job rate the same. When that cause and effect is so profoundly evident, that means that people who have up to now been pretty much stone materialists are not able to enjoy themselves as much and feel that maybe life is a little empty if it costs all that much to maintain an artificial boom going on.

While I was in the Marine Corps in Korea, my father sent me as much money as he thought he was getting extra on account of the war. He said he didn't want to make money on me being in a war.

An article in the *New York Sunday Times* comes to the conclusion that the only thing that could possibly snatch this country, the world, the whole planet out of the hole is a vast spiritual renaissance and a great return to the soil and a return to simple living. I talked to the head of the security guard at the University of New York at Stony Brook, who said, "I've been thinking about this thing a long time." Stony Brook is one of those schools that has had all the riots and the windows kicked out and all that business happen. And the head of their security department said, "The only thing that looks like it's going to do it is for people to get some kind of a spiritual awakening and some kind of a return to something simple."

We've been to several colleges where we've said, "Most of the stuff you're studying is hogwash, and probably you shouldn't bother with it." And they say, "You're telling us that what we've got a whole life invested in up to now isn't worthwhile."

Perhaps. Everybody working at whatever job they're working at, going to school, whatever they're doing, has got to look at what they're doing and see is it one of those jobs that is helping out mankind overall or is it one of those jobs that is stepping on mankind a little to make it.

Now, I've been being a spiritual teacher for about five years now. The way it worked out was I was just talking to folks, folks asking me about Spirit, and maybe about tripping, and in time I found that I was doing the job of a parish priest, which scared me instantly when I first found it out or noticed it. Upon researching that question I found out that spiritual teachers are where you find them, and if that's what I seemed to be doing that I should do it. I know about kundalini yoga and chakras and energy and telepathy and astral projection and mind-reading and all that kind of stuff. But what seems to me to be important is the recognition that a spiritual agreement is necessary here and now between us younger folks and our parents—a re-establishment of trust.

Now, it seems that I've begun to understand how ritual evolves. I've been holding Monday Night Class for five years … took off a summer, that's maybe two hundred and thirty class meetings. We go through a certain set of changes just to find out what are we doing here, and can we really put our juice behind this, and the ritual is the questions and answers that we go through in discovering that. When there's a question thing happening, once in a while one of the questions comes up that everyone knows is a heavy one, it's one of the ones that tell is it inclusive or is it exclusive, something that tells you a real thing about what kind of a trip it is. I'd like to go on into that part and start getting into dialogue, because this is an open advertised trip, this is a cross-section of this town here. These are good people to talk to, so if you have a question or if you want to point the discussion in a direction, just raise your hand up pretty high so I can see it.

How we doing toward the back there, is that really working out there in the hallway? If you can, just come up closer, and if there's folks that are outside the front door that can't hear, have them come around the side doors here, they can hear in these side doors. Come up closer, don't be afraid to get close to your neighbor if you haven't been introduced, because we're going to get introduced.

*Q: Can anyone join the Caravan?*

You don't have to be driving nose to tail with the Caravan to be on the Caravan, because all you have to do is do what the Caravan is trying to do and you're on the Caravan, wherever you are. All we've been saying all the way down the line is that if you blow your motor in some small town, then your job is that town, and you're the Caravan taking care of that town until you get your motor back together. Also that we take responsibility for everything in our path as we come across the continent. In that fashion I say I'm going to go do a farm thing and a lot of folks say, "Hot doggy, I want to go do your farm thing." More folks want to go do my farm thing than can be on one farm. That's cool, we can have lots more than one farm, too. There may be more of us than we can put in one heap, but that's okay, it only takes a couple of hundred to get to critical mass anyway.

*Q: Is your thinking settled now?*

Certain ones of my ideas are always in constant flux because I'm learning them right out as I go along. I feel like the essence of Zen is to remember that it's a cut-and-paste universe. But I've got certain basics I don't doubt: that any religious function must be all-inclusive and may not exclude anyone … I never joggle with that one. If I'm running some equation in my head and it comes up that it's going to violate that one, I just junk the whole thing.

The other one is karma, that as you sow so you shall reap. Well, I've never seen that violated. I hear rumors at a distance, by hearsay, but I've never seen it be violated. So I have to say that my experience so far has been to go on what I see.

And I never doubt that ... that there's one totality, one All, and that you may not comprehend the All because that would put you outside of the All, and there isn't anything outside of the All or it wouldn't be the All. A few like that are ones that I use for tools—like I don't doubt my crescent wrench. But any situation that comes up is capable of being re-evaluated until I discover where it's really at, and if I don't find the situation as groovy, then I try to dig into it and try to discover what's really happening. That sometimes requires doubt, changing your mind. You've got to be able to doubt and you've got to be able to change. If you can't adapt, you just freeze up in the system and you stop your spiritual growth, right there.

*Q: Why do you refer to people as monkeys?*

Because that's so far back down the line it's pre-sectarian; it doesn't have any racial, religious, or sectarian discrimination in it. We're pretty obviously self-evidently some kind of fancy evolved monkeys. Here we are.

The Spirit is here, there's no question about that. As for me I'm a medium trying to keep my message straight.

*Q: When you first started to live the life you're living now after what you had been, did you find it difficult to do?*

At some points more so than others. For instance I found that I could give up being a freshman English teacher at San Francisco State College real easily; it was just no trouble at all to do that. Other things, like I quit drinking milk, which had been my thing all my life. Instead of eating I'd just chug-a-lug a quart and fly on, and so that was one that got to me. I found that quitting milk was much harder for me than quitting acid. Acid I just don't have any regrets, everything is just per-

fect. Occasionally I want a glass of milk. The thing is to come from being a materialist to being based in Spirit.

*Q: If a person wants to live the way that you're living now but has his whole life looking back at him telling him not to, how do you think he should go about making his decision?*

I dig the sudden school. In Zen they say there's a sudden school and a gradual school. Somebody from the gradual school went to the teacher of the sudden school and asked him what was the difference between the gradual school and the sudden school and he said there wasn't any difference, there was no such thing as the gradual school, some folks were just quicker. It's how quick you want to be.

Here's the thing about cutting loose from the society: I'm both a free citizen and don't belong to anything and at the same time am a profitable member of this society. If I saw a forest fire I'd report it, I help out at scenes of accidents, whatnot, I'm like a valuable Boy Scout. But at the same time the reason I don't get in trouble with this culture is not because I obey this culture's laws, it's because I obey my own laws, which are much stricter than this country's laws in most instances.

I still want to pursue this thing, because it's an important place. You can do what I'm doing where you are right now, and it'll turn heavy.

*[Q: unintelligible]* Here's the thing, we monkeys are so many of us that we've got to have some kind of organizing principle or we're going to be just a mess, and so we make certain agreements. Like I drive on the right side of the road because that's the agreement.

*Q: ... Did you ever try driving on the left instead of the right?*

Only in England; I support the agreement. I try to make the road safe not only for me but for other folks.

*Q: ... Well I wouldn't drive then, if I couldn't drive on the left side if I wanted to.*

I don't want to. There's a question of Christian freedom. In San Francisco there's a place where this one street comes up to the entrance to a tunnel, and then you can't go in the tunnel because it's a streetcar tunnel, and you've got to turn left. You're in the left lane, and if you pull up to that thing and you want to turn left and you're in the left lane and the sign says, Left Lane Must Turn Left, and that's what you want to do, that's Christian freedom.

There's a Zen thing that says, "Before I attained Zen mountains were mountains and rivers were rivers, when I attained Zen mountains were no longer mountains and rivers were no longer rivers, and after I attained Zen mountains were mountains and rivers were rivers."

One day when I was really stoned, just when I was in contact with the whole universe and I was digging the sunset that was happening, I thought, Why don't I just make it happen a little longer. So I reached to do that, to find out where that was at, because I was at the place where mountains were no longer mountains and rivers were no longer rivers. So I looked, and in order to look I had to create perceptors to look with, and I said, How does physics work? And I came from pure intellect out through things like $E = mc^2$ and thirty-two feet per second as my graspers to understand the thing out here I wanted to do something with. As I reached out through the normal laws of physics by which the whole universe operates, I saw the perceptors I used to understand it make me understand that I didn't want to change it, and mountains became mountains and rivers became rivers again.

[Q: *unintelligible*]  She's talking about the idea that language affects our thought and how does our language affect what happens to us.

Q: ... *That partially, but more fundamentally just that one concept that when you put a name on something you are separating yourself from it— us-them, me-it, I-it—and that it should have some effect on how you see reality or how you work around it or do you at all.*

I am you, for openers. I just flat am you, and that realization has come to me a number of times. One of the times it came to me, I looked at somebody, and I understood the nature of our relationship, and then I reached for language, concept structures—oneness, equality signal, and you-ness, brought them down and said, "It's like … I am you." So I don't find any dichotomy in that piece of it.

Now as far as labels separating oneself, when I'm sawing firewood with the crosscut saw, I like for there to be enough difference between my hand and the wood that I can tell which is which so that I know which one to put the saw on. See, that's a basic level of ego necessary to involve yourself in cutting firewood.

So I don't feel that you're separate from anything at that level. We're a transaction—you and the universe interact. We are all one in practicality—geometrically, topologically, physiologically—we're all one thing, we're this organism here on the planet, and us and the planet's one thing, too. And the planet and space is one thing. As far as working around it, you don't work around a feeling that you're alien—you don't feel alien. That requires knowing that you're pretty much the same as other people. Well, for some people that's a refuge, and for others a fate worse than death.

*Q: What do you think of psychiatrists?*

I think that shrinks are secular priests and that charging money devalues them as priests, too. A psychiatrist is supposed to have to do with your psyche, and your psyche is your soul whether they admit it or not.

*Q: … Do they have any value?*

That depends on your individual practitioner. Psychiatry is a school of magic, the study of the *I Ching* is a school of magic, the study of law is a school of magic, the study of the Tarot is a school of magic, the study of the Bible is a school of magic, and so the thing about a school of magic comes out to be that it depends on the teacher. If the teacher's cool you're liable to have a cool school. That goes for any discipline. Anybody comes to town to bring you any kind of a trip, check the trip out for basics. Is it exclusive and does it charge money are basics. Spiritual teaching is for free.

*Q: What about the depression?*

I feel that it's becoming the agreement. The spiritual revolution and the depression go together, for a start. The financial trip is the country having an ego death. See, the country's on this ego trip—it thinks it's the only country in the world— and so what it wants is more, and as more of mankind understands the situation, a depression becomes the agreement.

*Q: What about the return to the simple way of life? Do you feel that it's necessary just to maintain the spiritual vow you've taken?*

The thing about returning to a very simple way of life is that my way of life may seem simple, but it's infinitely rich and varied and it's all I could possibly ask for. I don't even find it so simple. The world of the Spirit is very heavy, very complex, very beautiful, very simple, very real, very immediate—not something that you feel like you're being primitive if you're living a spiritual life. I eat good, I get to wear warm clothes, my roof doesn't leak on my bed.

*Q: ... But do you feel like you have to give up modern conveniences if you want to maintain a spiritual thing?*

It's going to get ripped off us by the universe anyway, so you ought to let go of it gracefully. Most of the people in the world eat the same thing every day, do you know that? Most people in the world don't eat meat, because they just can't afford it, they ain't got it. It's too ecologically unsound to get it up. It's a question about simple life with material and Spirit. In the material thing you experience things, and then you have to have a place to put your things when you're not experiencing them. Then you have thing-storage problems; it gets into other people going to get your things while you're not using them. You've got to lock up your things, keep other people from getting your things. Some people have things, some people want things, some people don't have many things.

There aren't enough Cadillacs to go around. There's enough rice to go around, but there aren't enough Cadillacs to go around, and in fact if you get too many Cadillacs it begins to cut into the rice supply. Then there's the idea that some people can't have a Rembrandt or a Picasso—some folks just have to do without. But any human being, if he puts out enough juice and wants to, can know Truth, which is heavier than owning a Rembrandt. That's not something that should make you feel deprived.

*Q: Could you explain some of your healing methods?*

Life force, or Spirit, or energy, or juice, is as you perceive it in your body. You can tell when the energy's on or when it's not on. When you have a lot of energy on, you can heal with your touch, but don't be conceptual about it, recognize that there's got to be energy transfer. Sometimes I can make somebody's cold get better just by hugging them, like just hug them and split fields with them and give them some of my energy, and they'll come up to a higher energy level where you don't have colds. Having a cold is a function of a lower energy level.

If somebody's hurt, like a cut or a wound or something like that, you can put your hand over it to seal up the leaks that energy is leaking out of. You hold your hand there a while and your body seals itself up so it doesn't leak energy anymore. If you plug the energy leak, then all you have to do is keep it clean and it will heal rapidly. That's what shock is like, when you get pale and weak and trembly and so on. That's because your energy's all run off. Just by the act of putting your hands over a wound you can stop the energy from leaving, and help that person toward healing by keeping them strong, not letting them get weak in the transaction.

Just by keeping your vibes good you don't catch many diseases, because you stay too high on top of it. Also if you can understand the beginning of an ailment ... now ailments are diseases, dis-ease. What you do for dis-ease is you ease it, you relax it. The way you relax it is you add energy to it, because it's tight, because it's not got much energy in it. So if you can get to where you could rev up that energy in yourself and just touch people, you can help them out a lot.

*Q: What are ego agreements?*

A lot of times people will help you get away with things that aren't cool. That's ego agreements. You've got to watch an ego agreement—it's a game. No agreement at all has its level of manifestation, and an ego agreement can come on heavy to no agreement. Then a spiritual agreement can supersede an ego agreement.

One of the reasons the stakes are so high right now is religion is in the process of trying to get folks into spiritual agreement. There hasn't been such a huge agreement-producer as television previous to now, but there's getting to be masses of ego agreements among people. There's got to be a strong spiritual agreement to help bring the cosmos through this trip.

I think we've come to a good agreement. I think we should secure this meeting because it's in a good clean place to do that. Let's OM just a little bit to put our heads in that frame to take home with us.

*And when we got down to Washington, DC, we parked the buses on the oval in front of the White House.*

SUNDAY MORNING SERVICE, WASHINGTON MONUMENT
WASHINGTON, DC
27 DECEMBER 1970

ust stepping out in front of you makes me warmer.

First Sunday after the solstice. More light. We turn on through the longer days. I was thinking this morning that praying is like communicating telepathically, and praying to God is like communicating telepathically with God. And you can pray with your fellow men. I felt like we were praying this morning right here in the middle of the city, the capital of the country, in some ways the capital of the world. I thought of things that I had heard in speeches given by all the men that had been presidents and whatnot all my life, starting with Roosevelt, and they always say, "Pray for understanding." And I found myself there looking over at the lit-up Capitol Building and thinking, Pray for understanding!

We didn't ask to come down here, by the way. I just thought it was reasonable that American citizens ought to be able to come down to the Washington Monument and dig a sunrise. I think that anybody we talk to and anybody we come in contact with will think that we're really reasonable and that we ain't scary.

I told the park police that we'd probably be around till at least noon, so we should probably go over and fire up our stoves and have breakfast and whatnot, huh? I don't think anybody has any questions at this temperature. Let's go get warm then ... and hang out. We can hang out here in this center of the thing for a while.

God Bless you, thank you for a really stoned morning ... so beautiful.

*Narration:* With a lifestyle all their own, one group which has found something different recently completed a cross-country trip in some old school buses. The travelers are now in Washington, where CBS reports.

*Interviewer:* It's a strange Caravan, fifty school buses repainted and remodeled to house a communal group which left San Francisco on Columbus Day to discover America. The group called the Monday Night Class has made its way coast to coast, each night pulling into a park or shopping center, school or church parking lot. There are about two hundred and fifty members making the trip, about forty of them children. They've been taking odd jobs along the way to pay for food and gasoline. At each stop wood is collected for the small stoves which heat many of the buses.

The group claims a varied membership, including teachers, students, engineers, a pilot, a lawyer, a carpenter. Three babies have been born so far on the trip, delivered without assistance from doctors. Two more are due any day. The class is held together by a philosophy blending bits of various religions. Members feel friendliness, and their belief in self-help and nonviolence have overcome a long-hair-and-beard stereotype among middle Americans they've met, even if some of their ideas, such as the use of marijuana and the hallucinatory drug peyote, have yet to win acceptance.

*Stephen:* I had not been raised religious and had no religious upbringing and I was on a completely materialistic trip and had done what you do if you're going to be a good materialist. I was kind of a Bertrand Russell agnostic, going to be one of the good guys even if I didn't believe in God. All that kind of thing. And I went to school and got a degree and was a good boy at that level. And then I suddenly saw that a whole realm of existence that I had dismissed as superstition was really not only real but was what determined what happened to the rest of it. It blew my mind. I realized that there was stuff in the Bible that was just literal truth—that the Sermon on the Mount is not just goody-goody Boy Scout instructions but a technical manual on how to survive.

*Interviewer:* Each Sunday morning the class holds its form of religious services. This morning the adults and a few children went to the Washington Monument at dawn to meditate and watch the sunrise. As these modern gypsies prepare to swing through the South and head home to San Francisco, they speak of getting farms, building cabins, and growing what they need to eat. Their plans may be naive and they admit few of their number know anything about farming, but they say they knew nothing about driving and maintaining buses before they set out to discover America their way.

The thing about the OM that I like best is that it always makes me remember what I came here to say. Sometimes I have trouble remembering, during the week or when we're driving a long time, or when we have to spend a long time hustling a parking place, but always when a bunch of folks do the OM I remember that we're all really one, and it's really important that we come together and affirm that and say it's really real. The vibration that we created in the OM is a religious statement. The nice thing about the OM is it's completely wide-open monkey—nonsectarian. It doesn't belong to anybody. Now it starts off like I want everybody to know and to be comfortable in their Universe. I want everybody to know Spirit. And that's sort of like a long time out there.

The state of enlightenment is something like being a grownup and being sane, and recognizing the responsibility to everything else that lives. So then I get off into the idea of being a little bit nutty. What kind of nutty? Usually ego nutty. That's what nutty is, ego, when you get right down to it.

There are kinds of nuttiness that are more than just dishonesty or ego. There are genetic and chemical kinds as well, that need medical help. Even those kinds can be helped by being a good honest tripper.

You start finding out that there are some things that Freud and the Catholic Church and the peyote Catholics in the southwestern United States all have in common—that the rites of man, the things that man needs to do with his fellow man to get it straight, are the same for any kind of man anywhere.

Now you folks that came here came from a cross-section of causes. Some of you came because of the *Washington Post*. And some of you might have caught the thing on television. Some of you picked it up word-of-mouth down through the beatnik community. Some of you are parents of people in the Caravan. Some of you are alert Washingtonians going to keep up with the latest thing, find out what's happening. Got some of them tonight. Well, that's enough representatives that we could call this the Astral Continental Congress.

There's also a bunch of people here who know what I'm about, know what I'm doing, and came here specifically for the purpose of getting stoned and going into telepathic communication with me.

How about that? Isn't that pretty? Isn't that a pretty vibe went on then? That was really nice. Now that place that we're in ... this is a

communion here now. Notice the quality of vision. How many people will raise their hands and cop to that telepathic phenomenon we just went through? Far out.

Now the energy that we create is what they call human grace. There's God's grace, which is free, and there's human grace. This is a church; presumably it's already got a store of human grace, if people come to it reverently to worship. That means they charge up its electricity. We as a culture have been led to believe that talking is our only form of communication, and in a court of law we're held to a stenographer's transcript of the verbal plane. And the justice or injustice is decided on that level. They talk about the letter of the law, and the spirit of the law.

*There were a couple of unusual incidents that happened to Caravan members while we were in Washington, DC. This story is from Michael T.*

*We had awakened before dawn to a knock on the side of our bus. In the dark, we maneuvered the entire Caravan, fifty or so vehicles, out of our church parking lot, through the deserted streets of DC, and over to the Ellipse, a park area between the White House and the Washington Monument. Most of us stayed in bed as long as we could, our vehicles moved by designated drivers and navigators.*

*Most of us knew we wouldn't have done this if it weren't the Washington Monument, and two days after Christmas to boot. It was just one of those moments, full of meaning and symbolism, pregnant with possibilities .*

*After the service we did retire to our buses to warm up and have breakfast. Some of us crawled back into bed for a while. Our group had a special treat for the day: peyote, the psychedelic cactus that Native Americans had been using for centuries to gain insight into life. About mid-morning, several of us were sitting around on the bed platform of the Freeway Flyer sipping peyote tea, munching popcorn, and talking over the state of the world. We were catching up on the events of the last couple of years and coming on to the peyote when a knock came on the bus door.*

One of us answered, and in stepped two young men, one African American and one Caucasian, in full uniform. These were Department of the Interior police, federal officers. The Ellipse and Washington Monument are part of a National Monument area, which, like our National Parks, is federal property and under federal jurisdiction.

The officers were polite and friendly. We invited them to come to the back of the bus and talk to us. We exchanged pleasantries. We told them what we were doing on the Caravan, our purposes, our goals. And, after a little while, we told them what it was we were sipping, and invited them to share some with us. Both men accepted, and they sipped peyote tea with us. We talked for a while longer, and then they had to go, to get on with their rounds.

Before they left I said to them, "By the way, aren't you unusual for federal officers? I mean, most of your fellow officers would not have shared peyote tea with us, would they?"

"Oh," one of them replied, "we're the liberals on the force." They smiled, we shook hands, and they left with a final wave and a nod of their heads.

Several times on the Caravan Stephen had told us that we were living at a very unique time, a crossroads, an unusual moment in history. So much change was happening, people felt so confused and so desperate, so hungry for understanding, that a window was temporarily opened into their hearts and minds. People would listen to new ideas, consider points of view they would not have considered before. We had a chance to influence our culture, the group mind of America and the world, in the direction of peace and compassion and living with nature rather than trying to dominate. That's why we were doing this Caravan. But we had better act quickly, Stephen would tell us, because the window might soon close, the culture harden up again.

And it was working! Everywhere we went, the authorities and the mainstream society as a whole were very sweet to us, treated us with a great deal of respect. We had the highest spiritual and ethical standards, went out of our way to be and appear harmless, to show respect to others, to work hard and not ask for handouts. All this worked in our favor, but it wasn't just us. It was partly the times.

But on that cold morning in Washington DC, these officers, both of them clean-shaven and squeaky-clean, were just doing their job. They were making their rounds, checking us out. They KNEW we were harmless, and treated us as such. Their department is to be credited with sending in the young liberals rather than some crusty old hard-liners, who might have made us feel threatened or even provoked an incident. They knew enough to handle the situation with the least possible flap.

But beyond that, these officers, and by implication, their department, respected our rights. Stephen was right about that. We were American citizens visiting some of our treasured scenes, we were clearly no threat, or even a bother, to anyone, and so, beyond checking us out, which was their job, they not only left us alone, but made us feel at home.

And even beyond that, these two particular individuals chose to join us in a ritual of peace. They didn't have to do that. They could have ignored the peyote and moved on. The fact is, they LIKED us, trusted us enough to know that we wouldn't hurt them. And we certainly weren't going to tell ... By that gesture these officers let us know their sympathies were with us, even though they could not necessarily expound upon that while in uniform and in public.

So here we were in one of those magical symbolic scenes that seemed to happen throughout the Caravan: a black man and a white man in uniform, sharing a heavy sacrament with a bunch of hippies on the Sunday morning after Christmas and the solstice, in the heart of the capital of the world ...

There is a phenomenon which you can perceive, which can show you, for your own self, the existence of Spirit. The presence of Spirit can be felt by anybody.

Then questions come like, "Why bother about the presence of Spirit, what is that going to do for us? We got Vietnam and we got housing and urban renewal, we got hard dope and racism." In this room right now there are probably people who lean toward the idea that, to the extent that I'm spiritual and not political, I'm taking people out of the political movement.

Then there are people on the other end who aren't familiar with Spirit and wonder if you have to have some kind of special knowledge to feel it.

There are some things I can tell you about because I can see them, because I see a lot more stuff than I used to see. I have vision of other planes than the material. Now that sounds weird and mysterious. You know, every time I say that, I try to say it in a different way so it won't sound weird and mysterious. But it's not weird and mysterious, and all the religions of the world cop to other realms of experience and other planes of existence.

We as a species, as monkeys, need to talk among ourselves and find out where it's really at. It looks to me from this position, and I've been doing things like this for about five years, that a great co-operation is the only thing that can pull humankind out of the hole we are in. I went from a place of political ignorance to political awareness.

The Democrats think there's a class war. They think class war has taken away the benefits from the old people and taken away the educational opportunities for the youth and taken away the benefits for the veterans and taken away the benefits for the veterans' wives and that we live in a time when the families of soldiers in combat are living on welfare. The Republicans think class warfare is when the Democrats mention any of that.

Any system is cool if the people in it are cool. We try to learn how to get cool, and we want to come out and communicate with other people that want to get cool. I'm not an escapist. We're householder yogis. If you figure out where it's at, what you'd better do is tell the person next to you, or help them find out. It looks to me from the state of the thing that we need a bunch of folks who know where it's at.

*Q: What is beauty?*

I think that for me beauty is that inner illumination that you see in people who are good. I don't mean that you can arrange your face into a certain shape, because beauty does not depend on the shape or anything like that, it depends on soul. It depends on being lighted from within—that's having a lot of energy on. The only way you can dependably have a lot of energy on is to have good karma. And to know you have good karma, well, you have to have had good karma for a while to know it.

So I think people get beautiful. I've seen people who when I first met them weren't beautiful in their superficial appearance. Actually I don't see any difference in folks at all. Because anybody I look at, I can tell whether the one I'm looking at is the best one they've got or not. And if it's not the best one of them they've got, then I want to see it. I'm going to keep hassling them until they tune up and let me see the best one they've got.

That's another difference between me and a preacher kind of a teacher. An American preacher type is supposed to stay back with the women and children. And I don't think that's where a teacher ought to be. I think he ought to be out talking to folks, and if some dude's got bad habits, hassle him about it some, you know? You've got to have a certain amount of hassle in the universe anyway; you might as well use it profitably.

*Q: What is stoned?*

I think that's a really legitimate question. What is stoned? Is it desirable? Now there's various kinds of states that people put their heads in. I remember the first time I found out that drunk and stoned was different. It was at my twenty-seventh birthday party. I got kind of telepathic on some grass, and everything turned golden and it was beautiful, and I said, "This is really different from drinking." Well since then I've found out a whole lot more about it.

Being stoned charges your energy field. There's things that happen if the energy field is highly charged. For instance you're smarter and better-looking, just turned up into a better one of you, all the way across the board, if that field is charged up. We have a word for that in our language: graceful. Being graceful is being full of grace. That just means that your battery's topped off good with Spirit. And beauty … being stoned makes you beautiful, if you're really stoned.

Now it turns out that there's lots of ways you can charge up your field. Grass will charge up your field. Chanting the OM like we just did will charge up your field. It got pretty stoned in here during the OM. Also that place where I said that some people had come here to be in telepathic communication was a very stoned place, for the record.

What is stoned, and why be stoned? Well here's the thing: Things like too many jackhammers, and too many loud radios, and too many loud cars, and too much driving around in motor vehicles all the time, and too much being scared about politics, and too much being scared you're going to get atom-bombed, all that kind of stuff brings you down. And bringing you down doesn't just mean changing your state of mind, it means that you lose your energy.

Another thing that keeps everybody from being high all the time is that they lose it through what I call holes in the bucket. Complaining is a hole in your bucket. If you complain, it just brings you down right away. Being jealous brings you down. Being angry brings you down. And when I say it brings you down, that's not an ephemeral mind state I'm referring to but your entire condition across the board. And you can see people go from pimples to clear skin in a matter of minutes, as their electricity changes.

How many people have seen anything at least that dramatic go on behind being stoned? Yeah, it's really far out to have gotten to see that kind of thing.

Now as a culture we have a low energy level. Everywhere there's a spot of energy people just come flocking to it. There's a lot of talk about charisma lately. You know, a political dude's supposed to have charisma. That's being an energy center enough to attract people's attention, because people's attention will go to an energy center.

Because energy doesn't have to be as rare as it is, but it is kind of rare. We could have a lot more if we all started being really sane in our culture.

Now being stoned is on a continuum that goes from not being stoned into getting a little bit stoned, and then into getting real stoned, and when you get real stoned it starts changing on the same continuum, but on another level of it. It goes high, and stoned, and then after stoned it gets heavy, and then it gets awesome.

We're kind of a funny thing. I caught our newspaper things and our television things, and they made us look like we were this little tight commune which is out doing this thing. Well, we're that, but that's also our traveling convenience. We're like stage two ambassadors ... I want to show you some information. How many people who are on the Caravan are not from California? Would you raise your hands? You see? So that's the first stage of being an ambassador: They went from all over the United States to San Francisco.

And the second stage is, we all came out from San Francisco, representing still where we came from first. I'm from Colorado, but also representing something we found that we came back here to tell you all: Know that Spirit and energy determines matter, not that matter is what determines Spirit and energy—then you can do things that make a difference in the world. It isn't that we like grass, or even peyote, it's that we like to be stoned. And those seem to be the simplest ways we have found right now to be able to do it in this kind of a culture, because this culture doesn't respect being stoned in its overall cultural thing like individual people do. We never have any trouble with anybody we talk to face to face. Anybody we communicate with, they get high off of us, you know? We get 'em high. And they'd rather be high than not be high, because everybody knows where high is when they're high. Does that cover you some on that?

Q: ... It certainly helps.

Good, good.

*Q: Why did you ask how many people were sensitive enough to communicate telepathically?*

I'm always interested in how many people know they can. I really think that everybody can. In fact I know everybody can. But most folks have some subconscious, and subconscious is what blocks you from knowing that you're telepathic. I wanted to know how many folks knew we all experienced that thing together, no question.

That was a unanimous stoned that came on there, that's how come it was so really beautiful. But I asked how many people knew it while it was happening, because some people aren't watching their movie well enough to be able to answer questions like that, and I try to teach them, and I try to snap 'em up. I bet I could pick up a few people if I asked how many people since I asked that the last time have decided they also were in on it at that level. Anybody? Yeah. See? Quite a few more popping up. They thought it over and decided they were.

*Q: What do you teach in the Monday Night Class?*

Just what I'm doing now, just like this.

*Q: ... But this couldn't go on very long, you must have some particular text or reference work ...*

I must what?

*Q: ... Don't you have any text or reference works? I notice that you used a lot of yoga tonight, or spoke of it.*

Uh-huh. Well, I've studied as many of the world's religions as I've been able to gain access to. And what I find is that ... it's like when you learn one foreign language it helps you learn the next one. I first understood the nature of what was going on in an intuitive flash. And that was my first way of understanding—an intuitive flash in which I saw the way the thing works. Then I worked my way, as it were, through a yoga model, since the first person I found who talked that language was a yoga teacher. And I ran through that model until I could see my way through it in yoga terms. Then I could do it in Buddhism and Christianity. When I did it in Buddhism I found out about Zen, and I did fall in love with Zen somewhat, because Zen is so clean. It's a very clean and simple thing.

*Q: ... But if it's spontaneous, then it doesn't follow any fixed series, or lesson, or discipline.*

Well, the thing about all those religions is that you can stack them all up together like IBM punch cards, and you can look at them and see which holes go all the way through. And that's the trip we're trying to do, the one with the holes that go all the way through.

*Coming down through the south, we came into a rest stop outside Atlanta and parked. The media from Atlanta came out and said, "We're having a hard time in Atlanta, we've got a biker war on Peachtree Street, and things are pretty not nice in there, and could you help us out? Come on into town and see if you can help us out." We said we'd do what we could.*

*I started talking in a small storefront and then I was moved to a bigger building and a bigger building until by that evening I was in a fairly large building. And at a point, they said, "Why is our scene so bad?" And I saw something in the back of the room that piqued my interest, and I said to everybody, "Be real quiet for a minute and listen and see what you hear." And everybody got quiet and they listened real quiet to see what they could hear. And in the back of the room, the voice was very plain: "Speed, bennies, downers, heroin." And I said, "See? You've got trash dope in your scene. That's what makes your scene crazy and evil and not nice: Trash dope."*

PEACHTREE STREET
ATLANTA, GEORGIA
2 JANUARY 1971

eace and communion. It really feels like a good thing—to be here doing this on this street, in this town.

The way it feels to me is that you can just clear all your things and be in a perfectly empty vibration place and you can feel the city build up in you like background radiation, like a Geiger counter always goes, click … click … just because there's a certain amount of stuff going through all the time. Being quiet this way gives us the energy with which we can relax.

On the street we passed a kid selling mescaline and phenobarbital, and I went back and asked him, "How come Phenobarbital? What do you want to do that for? What do you sell that for?"

And he says, "'Cause people buy it."

I feel like Atlanta has a scene going on where they don't quite know what it is they're trying to do. They're maybe trying to be a little like Haight Street, but they don't quite know what it is they're doing.

I saw a thing going on out there—this may blow some minds, I hope—I was watching out there and there were four girls standing on the sidewalk, and two cops came by and one of them came up where they were blocking the sidewalk. They saw the cops come up and they acted like they didn't see them, acted like they weren't there until they got right up next to them.

And then the older cop said—and I have to say that his vibes felt okay to me—he said, "You good people move over so folks can go down the sidewalk," and a couple of them turned around and snarled at him, and he reached over and he touched a girl. He put his hand on her, and it was a compassionate gesture, but as soon as he touched her she went rigid and chilled on him and ripped him off of the energy he extended to her, and he turned around and he said, "Okay, okay, move on down the street." And I think what I just witnessed there was what some folks call an incident of police harassment. Does anybody understand what I'm talking about?

*Q: Couldn't that be typical people's prejudices, like they picture someone and say, "Well that's a cop, they're all bad." I find that all the time.*

I don't. It may be prejudices, but it looks like the dumbs, and there's a fellow standing on the corner selling barbiturates, and they get you dumb.

Now the reason I brought that thing up is because of feeling pretty cool and then feeling my stomach load up with hard vibes. How many people can feel that periodical thing happening? This is what yoga's like: When you learn to breathe good enough to keep yourself from being uptight, then you can put yourself on overdrive and try to breathe good enough to help other folks from being uptight. Why doesn't everybody move in close so that folks that come in can walk down there.

Now a Sufi teacher is usually a dancer, and his magic, called *baraka*, is transferred in the dance. Well, my home yoga is *raja yoga*, which is the yoga of making discriminations. I had to learn how to keep my attention in my bod, which is part of tantric yoga.

So the dance that I do is with my head, and so we build this exchange, and as it builds, certain implications become apparent from what's been said so far. Somebody or other's going to follow those implications out, because everybody knows what the real thing is. I feel like everybody knows where it's at all the time.

So as we make these exchanges the energy will flow with them, as it is doing ... What I feel now is that the vibes here are stoned but jangly. It feels a lot mellower in here since we settled down, and the street's beginning to mellow a little bit. A group of people this size has a vibrational effect that goes way out. We're affecting people several buildings down the way who are running quieter trips now than they were a little while ago, because it changes the whole atmosphere. Doesn't it feel good?

I think there are real questions that are relevant, so let's do those and have a dialogue here, because I think that's the thing that'll make us a strong vibe that we can sustain for along time on the street. Ask questions about something you really want to know the answer to.

*[Q: unintelligible]*  Okay. You know how a super-cooled solution works? You can take water and cool it until it's below thirty-two degrees, and if it's perfectly pure water it won't turn to ice. It will remain liquid, and you can chill it to way, way below zero without it turning to ice. But if you drop one crystal in it, it becomes ice right then, and the shape of the molecular structure of that ice is determined by the shape of the crystal that drops in it.

Now an example of how that works is in the snowflake. Snow-flakes have two characteristics: one, that they all have six sides, and the other one is that within that they're infinitely variable.

Well, the six-sidedness of a snowflake is $H_2O$—that's the shape of the structure of the molecules that creates the six-sidedness. The infinite variation is the specks of dust that they form around, which are all different. What's going on right now is that the country is a super-cooled solution for Spirit, and it knows it's super-cooled because it knows that there are so many people trying to move it in a direction, trying to be that crystal.

What we're out here doing now is we're trying to be an ice crystal of a kind and a shape that can integrate all of the things, but still make a snowflake that's acceptable for everybody. So there is a religious revival happening. We like to say that it has to be all-inclusive, may not exclude anyone, that it's got to believe that people have free will.

It's got to believe in as you sow so you shall reap. When you start thumbing down through religions you find some believe one thing, some believe another. We're trying to see which principles are common to all, and that's the shape we want the crystal to have, that the country's going to freeze on. So we're out doing that right now. We're out here throwing crystals, because it's so obvious that something needs to be done. I feel that this country needs, as a country, an ego death, and I think a depression is an ego death for a country.

I think it's already happening and they're trying not to cop to it, but you keep hearing about people that used to have fancy jobs that made a lot of money not having them anymore. The conceptual stuff that nobody notices is going to fall off first. Then farther on down the line it'll start getting into folks where they'll have to get together and share for there to be enough, and that's fine, because I think that as the material plane does its thing then the spiritual plane is going to gain more value.

The thing about the pilgrims is that they were an ice crystal and they flavored the country, but unfortunately they were carrying guns, and this country was based in violence. It was conceptually based in justice, but it was materially based in violence. That's where it's at now, conceptually just and materially violent.

So we're reaffirming. This is the second American Revolution, the revolution of the soul. They said that you couldn't enslave a man's body, but they left it open that you could enslave his soul. And you've got to say you can't enslave his body or his soul. So we try to be a good-shaped crystal, like the pilgrims, but not carrying guns.

Q: *How do you make it?*

We stay into high enough energy that it doesn't bum us to work, that we can work and dig it.

Q: *... But in India there's not enough work for everybody, is there?*

Not enough work? There's always enough work; there's so much that needs to be done. There's just a ton that needs to be done if folks just up and do it. I think that folks spend a lot of time waiting for a contract before they'll work. But if you just up and do it, it starts flowing. We tried for three or four days to get a meeting off in this town, and we just kept working at it and talking to people.

There were rumors all over the place that there was going to be a meeting. We wanted to meet in this room and that room, but we couldn't connect with anything. It didn't happen until we went to another building and settled down and started having a meeting and got the juice up, and then this happened.

I feel like everybody wanted this place enough that they got it, that it was a good thing for them to have. I think that no matter how funny the world is you've got to know that that's the agreement. So the question then becomes obviously to change the agreement, doesn't it? If the agreement is now that it's okay to waste people on the other side of the world as long as you don't waste them up where you can see them, I'd just as soon chuck that agreement—it isn't a fair agreement.

*Q: ... I'd like you to talk about your group's group head, and about Atlanta's group head.*

Okay, I be part of a lot of group heads. A marriage is a very tight group head. And then the whole Caravan is a group head. The thing about a group head is that a group head runs by the same rules that an individual head runs by, so a group head can get schizophrenic, just like an individual head. Or a group head can go on an ego trip, just like an individual head can. The thing about a group head is if all the folks in it are paying attention, you can keep yourselves pretty straight by sharing your stuff.

Now non-communication among the members of a group head is the same thing in a group head as schizophrenia is in an individual. Schizophrenia in an individual is when the individual is alienated within himself. In a group head it's just that folks aren't talking to each other. Now we have a bunch of folks all here in this room, which makes us a group head, and we're pretty much all paying attention to the same thing, so it's a pretty focused group head.

You could have this many folks in here, one of them reading a magazine, and one of them writing on the wall, and doing all different things, and even if the folks were all doing different things it would still be a group head. That's just the kind of group head it would be, a random one. Now Atlanta is a group head. It's stoned, no question about that—there's energy running all over the place out on the street—but there are really lots of directions happening.

I call people monkeys a lot. It's something about a group head; it's because I don't want to cop to any smaller group head than all of us finally. I like to say monkey because that's previous to being an American, and that's previous to being Homo sapiens, and that's previous to being Chinese or any of that stuff. We're all monkeys.

*Q: I agree that Atlanta's a city where all the energy's there but it's flowing in all kinds of different directions. What I'm very interested in is bringing it into focus, and what ideas do you have on this.*

Well, here's the way a scene comes into focus. If you ever watch a kid learn how to talk … they don't learn grammar and then pronunciation, or they don't learn vocabulary and then structure or something like that. The whole thing comes into focus like tuning a microscope— it just all comes into focus at once. Well that's the way a scene works.

A Zen master I know says, "If it's raining out, don't bother walking faster, it's raining everywhere." So the scene we have going on in here is attentive, but it's not too peaceful yet. Well that's because the walls don't stop anything that's real, because we are also those folks driving by outside.

We are also the people in these buildings all the way out there, and we are also the people walking up and down out there. So some of us are sitting in here paying attention, and some of us is not. That's recognizing the group head as it really is, without the barrier of space or time, because there's no space/time barriers to telepathy … to the thing that connects us all and makes us all be one.

I felt a lot of people understand that and the vibes get better in here. The vibes got looser and easier in here, I feel like, because some folks are realizing that the first thing you have under control is right here, and if you make yourself peaceful ... feel it come on stoned at that place? Now when we're doing a thing like this we're being an open energy valve. When we relax and be open we're letting energy from higher planes into the system. All that's ever wrong with the system is low energy—let enough energy into the system and it's groovy, everybody digs it again. It gets into low energy, and nobody likes it.

*Q: I was wondering about control and decisions on your bus and on your whole Caravan. How is that done?*

It depends on what we're deciding. We talk about everything and we all understand it. I never told anybody to get a bus. I never told anybody to come on a caravan. I never said any of those things. People do a lot of outrageous things for me, hard yogas. But I very seldom ever assign one to anybody.

Once in a while I just might figure this fellow, this is what it takes, and say, "Hey, man, you ought to be on a seven-day word fast, and don't say anything for seven days." When I do that for somebody, they don't have to do that if they don't want to. But if they do do it, they'll find out that seven days of keeping your mouth shut does a thing to your head. It'll really do it.

Anybody can do that. They say, "How do you do it?" And I say, "I don't know very many ways, but one of them is this way." Sometimes we stop and we'll just hassle it out, however long it takes, and sometimes I expect to be able to say, "Let's do it now," and that we can move. It's the trust we establish by hassling it out that makes it so I can say, "Let's move now," and everybody moves, because we move out of trust. If I lost my trust I could say, "Let's do it now," and nothing would happen. That's the inner meat of the question.

*Q: Have you lost any buses?*

We have a bus still trying to find the crankshaft for a '46 International in Davenport, Iowa. We've had other buses drop behind for weeks and get it back together, get their motor together and catch up. There's folks join the Caravan and leave the Caravan all the time.

I discovered when I first started having meetings that the only way you could have this kind of meeting would be if you did it like the old Zen monasteries used to do it way back two or three hundred years ago, when it was an open meeting and any wandering monk who came to the meeting was allowed to ask the master of the monastery questions, and if the questions were good enough questions it might get to be his monastery.

I figure that's the only way a thing goes, so that's why I always like to deal with an open door both ways—free will. I don't want anybody around me that don't want to be around me, because that would just be a thing in the vibes. It wouldn't be cool. So all in all it's a matter of agreement as to how it works.

*Q: What's the purpose of the Caravan traveling across the country?*

We're coming out mostly, it turns out, to talk about peace, like being peaceful. I always like to talk about enlightenment because it's a rare thing in this century—a rare thing in any century actually—but we have a chance at getting into a bunch of it these days. But to talk about enlightenment, I find that first I've got to get an area around me clean enough of bad vibes that you can talk about that kind of thing.

So then it comes to you've got to talk about peace as a prerequisite. So we came out to share what we found because we found something that works good for us—to try to bring back respect for the idea of peace, which is a little disrespected these days, a lot of folks being into dynamite and whatnot.

We came out to visit our parents, because we're from all over the United States and we figured one of the things we had to do to get cool was to get cool with our parents. So we've been making a try at it, stopping by and talking to them and finding out if we can get it together. And we can a lot of the time.

Most of us have been able to connect with our parents, and there are parents coming out from all over to visit us. We had folks drive up from Florida to meet us here, because this was the closest we were getting to where they were, to come see their children and come meet their teacher.

A lot of parents come in to see me saying, "Where you going with all our kids?" I feel like I've got to talk to those folks as long as they're being straight with me and trying to find out that answer. So we're doing that, being that.

Also we're being an audio-visual example that we can, in these buses, drive all around the United States, circumnavigate that thing, camp on the White House lawn and whatnot, and can do that thing in 1970 and 1971 in the United States … that we are able to do it. That's relatively fancy in itself, I think. So that's what we're doing is out trying to show that the human contract must not be breached, that we must maintain enough trust among us to do anything at all.

When we first came here we had Atlanta television out to see us, and those fellows had the wire services plugged in on one ear and the teletype in the other ear and whatnot, and what they said was, "Can't you stay in Atlanta awhile?"

I said, "How come?"

They said, "Man, it's so hard. They been killing people. We need you here. Stay here and help us get the thing together."

Isn't that far out? That's because they had word from all the way back down the line how we've been being.

The only thing anybody's hassled us for, pretty much, is for, "Where you going to park all those buses?" So that's what we're out doing. Also we're learning a whole lot. One thing we learned is that you can drive for five hundred miles at a time in parts of the United States and not see anybody else. We've been up in places where there just aren't any people for as far as you can see in any direction, for miles and miles and miles. They talk about it being crowded and all that. It's crowded right around New York and right around Los Angeles, it's really crowded, and not much fun.

But you get out in the rest of the country and there's a lot of country left, and it ain't so bad. It's pretty good-looking country.

*Q: Were the American Indians violent people?*

The peyote Indians are nonviolent people. In fact one of the famous peyote chiefs was called Quanah Parker—the town of Quanah, Texas, is named after him. Quanah Parker was a famous war chief at first, and he was dedicated to the principle that the only good white man was a dead one. And he renounced violence after his first peyote trip.

The peyote Indians are nonviolent. Quanah Parker became one of the most famous peyote road chiefs after that; after having been a war chief, he became a road chief.

Another nice thing about peyote, by the way, that's interesting is that as well as the American Indian peyote churches there are black peyote churches, because there used to be tribes of runaway slaves. Enough of them would run away till there would be enough of them together to be a tribe, and some of them got into it with the Indians, interacting with them, and some of them got to be peyote Indians. They became like black Indians. And there were and are peyote road chiefs, black ones, Indian ones, and white ones, too.

I feel that if you can think of something to do that'll make you peaceful, do it, because the only way we're going to have peace is to BE PEACEFUL, right? You can't talk peace, you can't force peace, you can't do anything but be peaceful, and if you be peaceful you create peace around you.

I want to cut us loose there. Good night and God Bless you and thank you, Atlanta, for having us here to visit you. The Caravan should maybe gas up so we'll be ready to roll in the morning.

The hostess said she had invited friends and communications folks, and she kind of put the idea on me a little bit that she wanted me to talk about media. That's kind of a funny trip because I'm a medium myself in several senses of the word. Here's one sense that I'm a medium: Whenever I'm doing a class meeting, it's over when there aren't any more questions.

One night it looked like it was about eleven-thirty and we'd talked about everything that was important and I wanted to know if there was anything more important that had to be said before we could close the meeting. One dude put up his hand and said, "I want to know if anybody here knows Johnny, cause his friend in Mendocino wants to send word to him to say hello." At that point we had just become a completely pure medium and we had no business to take care of; that was the next message so I knew we'd taken care of our business for the evening. We were being a communications medium— just a room full of people is a communications medium—and then I'm a medium myself.

People ask, "What's the Caravan doing, what are you doing out here, why did you leave San Francisco, how come you came out on the road?"

Well, we want to talk on the international telephone to everybody, and it usually costs a great deal to get your international telephone hooked up. Some people do really strange things to get their telephone hooked up. We didn't want to hurt anybody, and we couldn't play guitar, so we figured that if you took about two or three hundred beatniks and dragged them all across the country ...

And where we've been going there has been a succession of people say, "Well, you may be able to get it on in this town, but, man, that next town down the road is tough, and they're going to lock you up soon as you come in the city limits." We've been from place to place all around the United States on that basis, and we're still going. The last place they said they were going to lock us up was Nashville; they told us that in Atlanta.

So that's a look at a medium. When Ringo was interviewed by an American magazine, in the course of the interview he told where his house in Surrey was and how much it cost and how much he'd accept for a down and all that, and just used it like the classifieds.

We've been getting a lot of practical experience in how pure are media, like how much difference is there between what you put in and what comes out on the other end. For a while we just did everything we could; we were going to control it somehow. We were going to say, "No more notebook interviews, you have to use a tape-recorder from now on." Then we saw what could happen to a tape-recorder interview. Then we thought, Okay, nuts to all the written press anyway, we'll just do television. That's the intersection of two senses; they can't blow that one too bad.

So we did television—we did a thing in Washington, DC, for the network. I guess we gave them enough material that they could have done about a three-hour spectacular on it. They had pictures of every bus on the Caravan, and all the kids, and they had long interviews with everybody, and they put it on the tube—two minutes and ten seconds, pow, zoom ... I don't know what you'd have to do about that. Television folks come up to me and say, "You got to understand it's a fast medium. You got to learn to be brief." Then they hold this thing up in my face and tell me I have twenty seconds and I say, "Uh, peace brother ..." because when you start compressing them down real close you start getting back to the classic ones.

When I was really young, maybe ten or younger, I used to notice that people could lie to each other and that that was one of the options—that folks had free will and they could lie, and that if you didn't know how to, you couldn't tell whether folks were lying or not.

I used to think that you were supposed to learn how to be a good poker player so you could check the other fellow out and see did he have the cards or not. I used to think how neat it would be if everybody just knew what everybody thought, and then there wouldn't be any lying.

It seemed to me that would bring a peaceful thing about, because it would be cool if everybody knew what everybody thought. That was kind of like a wish I had then, and I have to say now that my wishes are being fulfilled. The things that I wanted when I was a kid, my really sincere places, are just coming through. I think that's the way it is. I think it works that way, I think you get what you want.

When I used to think that it would be nice if everybody knew what everybody thought, I was really naive in a place because I didn't realize how heavy it would be if you could know what people thought ... that it could really be a far out thing. But I dismissed that as one of the possibilities, because it didn't look like it was real. Nobody had ever told me anything real about it. I just thought that would be a neat thing if people could do that, because it seemed like it would just really straighten out mankind, it would straighten out the whole problem.

Somewhere along the line, I guess when I was about fifteen, my mother sent me out to spend a year living with my grandmother in California because my grandmother could always make me put on a little weight and she wanted me to fatten up a taste.

When I got there I knew I could power-trip my grandmother into doing what I wanted her to, so I quit school and knew she wouldn't make me go back. I spent that summer reading a lot in the library, and I read what I could find on magic and voodoo and religion because I thought there was something happening in there. There was some kind of energy there, or there was something happening there, but I couldn't make it happen. I couldn't see how those things could make that thing happen.

Later, having given up on that, I put myself in for communication, and I was going to be a writer. Being a writer was just that I wanted to enter the communication flow. It wasn't that I wanted to write anything. I never did want to write stories, I never could write fiction, I never dug it. I didn't understand that I had to have something to say to write fiction.

Then I taught school. I guess at a place I was going to try anything because I'd done everything that you could do, it seemed; I'd done just whatever you could do and was right at a place where I was supposed to know where it was at and I didn't know where it was at yet. I was supposed to be telling people where it was at and I didn't know where it was at yet, and my students were leaving school and going off and hanging out on Haight Street and growing their hair out. So I went and did that with them.

The first thing that happened, after considerable messing around, was when Margaret and I were tripping together. We were looking at each other and she did something at me with her eyes and I felt something happen inside my head, and I said, "Can you do that again?" And she did that thing with her eyes again and I felt something happen inside my head, and I said, "Do that again." We were lying together on the bed and we just kept doing that, passing that back and forth, because I was afraid that if I got up to go to the bathroom or anything we'd lose that place.

As it went back and forth it got stronger, and we got to where we knew what was in each other's head, and we got to where we could look in each other's eyes and know knowledge back and forth. There's a telepathic communication where you say, "Hey, did you know that I just thought that just now?" And then there's the one where you don't have to say hey—the answer and the question go on the same channel. And we got to that place, and then she came inside my head, and her face appeared inside my head so I could see it in my mind's eye, and she became a cat and smiled at me, and my whole life changed.

Right on the spot my whole life changed, because that was the closest, most intimate communication that I'd ever had and it was the one I'd been looking for all the time. I didn't know I was looking for it, but when it happened I said, "That's it, that's the one. People can get to people." People can get to people ... something closer than the written word, something closer than the spoken word, something closer than gesture, something closer than touch.

You can just look in from mind to mind. At first, when I started coming on, I didn't realize what that was that we were doing, and I didn't realize the implications of it, but I just started studying it and doing it and getting high every chance I got and going to a place where I could be in communication with someone. And then in my studies of it I started thinking, Well wow, it's not as simple as I thought.

If everybody knows what everybody's thinking, that's one thing, but then what do you do about a political science or an etiquette for a territory where all the countries overlap, where all the countries don't have any borders. No space and time on that level at all.

And I started thinking, There's got to be some ground rules, because if you can do this with your mind you can do that with your mind, and wow, somebody could probably even cop somebody's head ... you know, get your gourd.

And I thought, Well there's got to be things to keep that from happening. I thought it looked like also there were places where wouldn't people on trips who thought they were heavy get together and get on power trips and things. Wasn't that one of the possibilities? So there had to be something about that, too. And so we tried to figure out what it was about, what it was like to be in that mental condition with other people ... what were the ground rules.

As we started inventing and creating ground rules, we had what we called our patchwork quilt. We started noticing that the ground rules that we created were quite similar to some other things that we had seen for a long time and didn't know what they were. What we started finding out was that the ground rules for telepathic communication are expressed in the Sermon on the Mount. What the Sermon on the Mount is about is the condition you have to keep your head in if you're going to be able to have company at all. That's the thing about telepathy—you've got to keep your head clean if you're going to have telepathy, because when somebody looks into your head it's nonselective, and they see everything you got. If you follow the implications of this idea you can have an understanding of the psychedelic experience deeper than most folks have.

There comes a place like this for me every time I try to talk to a bunch of people where everybody is gathered and I have everybody's attention and then I have to stop and look and see have I got anything worthwhile to say. And I have to go back and I have to think, Why am I doing this and what am I doing here, and why did we come out from San Francisco, and why am I talking to anybody anyway?

I guess it comes down to that somewhere along the line I found out that if you wanted anything done you had to do it yourself, and it looked to me that people could be treating each other better than they were on an individual basis, political basis, national, planetary … that folks weren't being as good to each other as they could be.

I had a vision once of exactly how the universe works. What I'm doing now is out testing that vision to see if that was a real one and if that's really the way the universe works. I saw that one person—anybody, if they were patient enough—could make a difference in the whole thing.

Now there's a story about Nikola Tesla—he's the fellow that nobody knows his name much but he's responsible for the alternating-current motor and generator and all vacuum-tube phenomena, which includes television and radio. And he was the fellow who knew about resonance … how if you pluck a G string on one guitar the G string on another guitar will resonate. And he went out one time to a giant steel suspension bridge across a really big river with a ball-peen hammer and a stopwatch. And he went over and he banged on the side of the bridge and he looked at his watch. Then he waited awhile, and a guard came out and watched him doing this for a while … and he'd look at his watch and he'd hit the bridge, and he'd look at his watch and he'd wait awhile and he'd hit the bridge.

The guard came over and said, "What are you doing?"

And Tesla said, "I'm going to tear this bridge down."

And the guard said, "Nutty old man," and went away back to the guard shack. And in a while, when the whole bridge was rocking and shaking on its foundation, the guard went back and called the police to come get this crazy old man who was tearing down the bridge with a ball-peen hammer.

And that's a piece of how the universe works, and we're testing that. I suppose somewhere along the line you will want to know who we are. Well, we're you who went to San Francisco, because somebody made a noise in San Francisco like there was something heavy happening there, like there was Spirit going on maybe. And a lot of people went out there looking for that.

And it was heavy, because there was Spirit there, and some other things. A lot of folks got hung up in the other things, but some of us kept looking for Spirit, so we don't feel like we're strangers anywhere when we got kin all over. And we're out with a ball-peen hammer, and we're going to fix the country. Now that sounds like we're going to do a revolution, doesn't it … that we're going to go out and change everything.

I feel that ever since there was a time when any man noticed that some folks were selfish and some folks were hungry there was a time for a revolution to happen. Well, I guess the first time anybody noticed that was probably the first time us monkeys ever had anything.

So they've been working it out for maybe, what, a hundred thousand years ... maybe it's been going on a lot longer than that but we just don't know about it. We've only got written stuff on it back about sixteen or eighteen thousand. And with that long a time to figure it out in, they said there is only one way you can really reach out and make changes happen ... that your revolution has to say that nobody is expendable.

There isn't anybody you can kill who could improve my situation. My well-being is not dependent on anybody else's absence. That's one of the criteria of a real revolution. It's got to be based on love and it's got to be based on truth. It's got to include everybody from in front. And there's a bunch of other things that go along with it, too. They've had them all put together and the revolution has been chomping on through for a long time.

We call it different names. We call it Zoroastrianism, and Buddhism, and Confucianism, and Christianity, and Judaism, and Islam. We're really in a far out place in history now. You can walk over to the paperback bookstand in the supermarket, and you can pick out, probably, the Holy Books of most of the major religions of the world. You can get into an understanding that there is more than one way to reach unity with God.

Now this here they said was a Unitarian Church. I almost don't keep track on that level ... in fact I don't keep track on that level. We've been in a Catholic Church, been in a Congregational Church, another Unitarian. Somebody said I was supposed to point out that although I was made able to use these facilities that I was not actually sponsored as such by the Unitarian Church.

Well I can make that statement, but on the other hand I don't see how I cannot be a part of the Unitarian Church. It says unit—that means one, right? There's only one Church and we're all in it. Unitarian means the same thing that Catholic means. It means All-

Embracing. When they speak of the Buddhist Church they call it the Universal Church. Like they got peace buttons and other kinds of buttons, but the one that's the button for this Church is your bellybutton, because everybody's got one.

Now I always knew that there were things I'd like to do to help out, but I never knew that you could, or that it was permissible. I found out that what you do about that is you be a grownup and you give yourself permission to just jump right in and start doing something. Now where I found that stuff out ... I guess some of that is from one of my early visions, but a whole lot of that is from what happened to me from trying to follow that vision. On my twenty-sixth acid trip, I had some lovely visions of the dance of the genes and the dance of the minds, which presented itself to me as a beautiful double-helix in my trip.

I think by now that I've already run out enough string that a lot of people have things that they want to ask. And that's where the real action's at is in the interchange, and any information that we need to know will come out in the interchange, too. So this is a chance ... we've been six or seven thousand miles by now, and we came out across the country to talk to you, so let's do that. Anybody who has anything they need to say that's relevant to anything here and now or wherever ... whatever is the business we got to take care of at hand, let's do that. Anybody got something happening right now?

*Q: I'm interested in what you have to say about different religions. I've been reading up on Christianity in the Bible, and some of the things in the Bible don't go along with what you're saying ... like when Jesus said, "If you're not with me you're against me," and, "Nobody comes to the Father except by me."*

That's a good question, but fortunately I have a good answer for it.

Although I am not a Christian I will tell you what I think. Jesus is the name of a man, and Christ is the name of a function. Jesus the

Christ is more accurate than Jesus Christ. Now when Jesus spoke, when he said "I," sometimes he meant, "I have to go out to the privy." He did, you know. You must never forget that, it's very important. And sometimes when he said "I," he meant the entire infinite. Now when he said, "There's no way to the Father but through me," he meant through that. Well, that is not particular to just Jesus—Jesus was born of woman on the planet and all that. This other Christness … Christ consciousness is a way to talk about that. Now I think that when Jesus said, "There's no way to the Father but through me," he meant that there's no way to the Father but by the consciousness of Christ—Christ consciousness.

Christ died because any time that the infinite (Spirit) binds itself to the finite (flesh, or matter), it ties itself to "thing law" and must suffer death. Christ consciousness is consciousness. Flesh without consciousness is brute and sinless and without free will. We monkeys who share life by the gift of consciousness must share the karma of Spirit in flesh and taste death.

*Q: … All religions say that they're all the truth and that they're the only way.*

Other people's religions should be respected if at all possible. The Holy Books I've read of many religions say you're supposed to study the Holy Books of all the religions and the teachings of all the sages impartially.

*Q: Right now, as I understand Western Christianity, I understand a system of God and an opposite to God, which is the devil.*

No, that's a misconception right there. The devil is not opposite to God. God has no opposite and is all-encompassing and there's only one.

Well, the material plane has its laws, the vibrational plane has its laws, the spiritual plane has its laws. If you're following the right laws for where you are, you're communicating with the universe in everything you do.

One time I went out to see my mechanic, and he had this giant black dog on a chain. And I said, "Hello doggy," and he charged out and he hit the end of the chain about six inches from me … Rrraarrr.

I just backed up and started to walk away from him, and the dude says, "Hey, I would like you to be straight with my dog, you want to be straight with my dog?"

I said, "Yeah, I'd rather be straight with him than this way."

So he said, "The first thing I have to tell you is that he's only mean when he's tied up."

So he broke him loose, and the dog came over and he sniffed my hand, and that was groovy. So I kind of grabbed on to his front teeth, you know, big fangs, and we started playing, and he'd pull at me and I'd pull at him. And it got to where it hurt my hand a little because we were pulling so hard. So I found an old sandal on the ground and gave him one end of it, and I got hold of the other end of it, and we started doing that.

And there's a way, if there's enough cooperation, that people who are disproportionate in size and strength can work out like through a gear-shift in the middle so you can both come on as hard as you can in the interchange. So pretty soon me and the dog were both coming on just as hard as we could … rraarr, rraarr, like that, and it got just really stoned, and a curved sine wave was going down my arm, through the dog's backbone and off his tail. And I realized right then that I was relating with the universe … and at that minute that sandal was a heavier means of communication than American Telephone and Telegraph.

And that made me realize that I'm relating with the universe when I feel what the front wheels of my bus feel like coming back through the steering wheel … and that however I do it on my end is how well I'm doing anywhere. I can't drive sloppy and say my head's cool.

I've got to put the same attention into driving as I do into meditating on some heavy old Zen text or something, same attention, because I'm relating with the universe all the time. Right now I'm relating with the universe here, however I'm doing this, however we relate.

*Q: The basis of Christianity is supposed to be immortality. What are your beliefs in immortality?*

I think that everything that we have goes on with the exception of the ego. The ego is an illusion. It isn't something real, so it can't be passed on. It's only a viewpoint. But everything else that is me never dies.

*Q. What about physically?*

Well, this machine that I have will run down, and all of my potassium will go back to potassium, and all of my phosphorus will go back to phosphorus, and all my life energy will go back to where it is. And a baby will be born, and there will be a need for some more life energy here on the plane, and there will be a drawing of $x$ amount of life energy out of the account to keep that baby alive with.

We are in a sense a three-part operation—body, soul and Spirit. The body, the meat part, is pretty obvious. The soul is the electro-tele-pathic-magnetic field that surrounds us. We have electrical stuff going on in us. Anywhere there's electrical stuff going on there's a field around it, like a magnetic field. Well that's our aura, and our aura is also our soul, because it's our extension as it goes out ... our other than fleshy part. Then there's Spirit, which is eternal, unchanging, unchanged always was, always is, always will be. Now that part always is, because it just always is.

Q: ... When you talk about always was, and is, and always will be, that's putting it into abstract terms. I want something that's concrete, something you can relate to the world from your own personal experience.

You want Spirit to be concrete. That's exactly the problem.

Q: ... How can we understand unless it's concrete?

Can you understand the multiplication tables? I'm saying that the multiplication tables are not concrete. They are abstract, it's in some-body's head. Look here. Here's a thing [holding up a photo], here's a thing [holding up another photo]. Well, a thing and a thing is the only reality. "Two" only exists in your mind, it isn't real. This photo is in no way connected to that photo. Just because you can put "two" around them like a parenthesis in your mind and say here's "two" pictures, that ain't "two" pictures. Here's a thing and there's a thing and they have their own thingness. You can't avoid abstractions if you're going to talk and think and do that kind of business. But you can experience. The only way you can get into concrete is by experience.

The thing about wanting Spirit to be concrete ... the body is thing, the Spirit is no thing, and the soul is the continuum between thing and no thing. So it's hard to get concrete when you've got no thing. But it's there and it's real. It not only is there and real but it makes the differ-ence in this part.

*Q: Yes, but we don't know that. Man is a temporal creature, limited, finite.*

Oh, only on one end. On the other end, infinite.

*Q: What methods do you teach for gaining this kind of consciousness?*

Methods I teach … One of them is to speak the truth in the here and now. In fact, speaking truth can be your handle to hold you in the here and now. We get spaced out of the here and now when we try to figure out half a truth or three-quarters of the truth because we can't put out a whole one. Just say a whole truth and accept what happens. If it's going to get you hit in the head, that's the way it goes. Say it because at least you'll be hit in the head in the here and now. You'll know where you're at. You won't be somewhere else.

*Q: About the discipline of the group … What if someone starts with good intent and goes part of the way and finds the discipline a little bit more than they can take, but you've moved them from where they came from and they have no place to go back to. What is your responsibility to those who drop along the wayside?*

Everybody is my student—those who leave the Caravan and those who stay. And what I try to do, and do do, is build it so people can get on or get off any time they want.

*Q: … I'm talking about those …*

People I kidnap and take out in the desert and kick out?

*Q: … People who were uprooted from whatever foundation they …*

No they weren't. They voluntarily decided they wanted to do something.

*Q: … They were stimulated to volunteer.*

You mean I'm an attractive nuisance?

*Q: … I wouldn't say that.*

You mean the part about the nuisance or the attractive?

*Q: ... I'm still concerned about ... you see, some of us actually have to stay in the play. What advice have you got to offer for the enlightenment of these United States?*

You got a subtle plane that just drips with stuff. You really do. I suggest, inasmuch as you're already in the racket, be a preacher.

*Q: ... Preachers don't do too good today.*

I don't know, man, I hear there's folks quitting preaching, but there's swamis and yogis flying in from all over the world because there's so much juice in this country for a preacher to dabble in if he wants to.

*Q: ... Do you have advice on how to do this?*

Oh yeah, just do it like it says in the book. Really, just like it says in the book. Sermon on the Mount is tripping instructions and will carry you through. If you have read the Sermon on the Mount so many times that it doesn't mean anything to you anymore, read the eighty-one poems of Lao Tzu and they'll tell you the same thing.

Read *Zen Flesh, Zen Bones*, it'll tell you the same thing again. It's all the same one, I'm not teaching anything different than anybody. It sounds different these days because I come along after Dewey ... what's that dude's name? Modern education ... John Dewey ... Well, I come along after John Dewey and Doctor Spock and a whole bunch of folks who saw a repressive culture and said, "Wow, back off, leave them alone, do your own thing." Well, we've been doing that for a while, now we're on the other side of it. Doing your own thing is groovy, but somebody's got to keep the toilet paper dry. So I teach responsibility.

I don't cop to fear and anger, or ignorance. I say that those are things that you can change.

Don't ever lock the door on somebody by saying, "Oh you poor ignorant thing." I always say, if somebody can do better, I tell them,

"You can do better." Because that opens the door. And if somebody gets a little juice, they can do better. You don't shut the door on them and say, "That's the best you can do, baby, you only got a 39 IQ." I don't believe in people being smart or dumb. I think that everybody is just as smart as anybody, only according to their condition and how much attention they're paying. And anybody can be as smart as anybody if they pay enough attention. That's the difference between religion and modern education. Modern education says, "Some of them, poor things, are problem children, poor things."

I feel that we're all really responsible for what we're doing. And that's freedom I bring by saying that, not repression. If you're responsible for what you're doing, no matter how bad your condition, you can change it. That's why I dig responsibility so much, because the other end of it is freedom. Give them freedom.

But as far as the folks that are going to drop off on the side goes, if they want to do it they can do it. If they don't want to do it they can do another thing, maybe we'll catch them next time around. But I don't think I'm leaving any half-broken hearts or anything like that. It's not that kind of a thing. Roots are not in dirt for us kind of plants. Our roots are in other people. And we're a good garden and anybody is welcome to grow in it.

I feel like I've about come around to where we should let go now. A couple of things … I'd like the Caravan to clean this building. Anybody who wants to come out to the park tomorrow morning, we're going to be out in the park in the daytime tomorrow out on Old Hickory Lake. Okay? God Bless you. Thank you for being here. It's been heavy and real, and I was really glad to come. See you all somewhere. Caravan's leaving Saturday morning. God Bless you.

*Interviewer:* Now you were in the Haight-Ashbury area.

*Stephen:* Before it got violent. I was there with the authentic flower children and I saw the rest of it, how it happened, and I watched all that go along as it did.

*Interviewer:* Was it good?

*Stephen:* It was really good. It was really fine. People were so trusting and so open and there was just a huge community that lived there and thrived, and we took psychedelics and went into each other's minds and got to know each other really deep. A lot of us got to a place where we could change the vision at will. We could change things in our heads and watch the things out in front of us change ... watch the vision change and that kind of thing. I just logged hours and hours and hours learning about the mind, because the first thing that happened to me when I came on to that level of mind was I found out there was a whole level of experience that I'd never been in before.

I'd never seen that, and people had been trying to tell me about it. They'd say, "There's Spirit, and there's magic," and a whole bunch of stuff like that. And I'd say, "No, man, that's all superstition. That happened two thousand years ago, not these days." But it was really happening, and as soon as I found out there was something like that, that was what I did on Haight Street. Most of the people on Haight Street were serious students studying mind.

Then it got to be where the symbols got important. We had a Human Be-In, the first Human Be-In. We count history from that in a way sometimes, because it was out of nowhere—thirty thousand people in San Francisco walked into a polo field and looked at each other and they all knew they were doing the same thing and none of them had known there was that many of them.

I remember walking up on the Human Be-In. I was about a hundred yards away from it and the vibrations were so heavy coming off that thing that my knees were shaking and watery and I had to stop and sit down against a tree for about ten minutes and come on to it like coming on to a psychedelic before I could even walk up to it.

And when I got there, I was standing looking down at that bowl full of people and there was a San Francisco mounted policeman there on his horse, and a lady came up to him and said, "My boy is down in there. Can you find him for me?"

And the policeman turned around to her and said, "Lady, all those people down there are smoking grass and if I went down there I'd have to arrest them, and I don't want to, so you'll have to find your own kid."

*Interviewer:* You say you were studying minds?

*Stephen:* Not minds, *mind*.

*Interviewer:* What did you learn? Was there something that came out of it?

*Stephen:* Yes. I found out that you can be telepathic, and the handles on it are in your mind. People used to come to me when I first started teaching and say, "Hey, man, I want to learn how to get telepathic, tell me the real thing." And I'd start off telling them and they'd say, "No, don't tell me all that goody-goody stuff, I want to know the real thing."

*Interviewer:* You can communicate mind to mind without speaking?

*Stephen:* In the right circumstances..

*Interviewer:* And the way to do it is to have moral structure?

*Stephen:* Yes, it's to be a moral person. Like to be a moral person means you can get to where you don't have any subconscious, and subconscious content is the only barrier to telepathy. See, I'm some a psychologist and some a spiritual teacher, but I find that *psyche* means *soul* in Greek, so a psychologist ought to be a soulologist instead of a rat torturer.

*Interviewer:* So when you're trying to get with someone else's mind, you try to be the best kind of person consistently that you can possibly be?

*Stephen:* Right. You keep your head clean enough that you don't mind having company in it.

*Interviewer:* And did acid help you do this?

*Stephen:* Yeah, it taught me how to see that level. I hadn't even been aware of that level, but it taught me how to see it and to understand it so I could look at someone and I could tell … sometimes I could tell how their mother toilet-trained them. I could see how their whole mind structure worked. I could see if they were jealous or if they were angry at me or if they believed what I was doing.

*Interviewer:* And you could only do this under the influence of LSD?

*Stephen:* At first. See, that's the thing. First I thought it was a science fiction trip. I used to read telepathy science fiction…. The thing is, is that it's so stoned in here now I can barely talk as we're going along here just on the vibrations of this, because I've found out that when you're cutting a tape for a lot of people it's just as heavy as if it's live, because the connection is made with the intent.

*Interviewer:* Well, don't let that bother you now.

*Stephen:* It's okay, it's not bothering me any, I'm just sort of floating in it.

*Interviewer:* All right. Now, Stephen, when you … after a while you learn how to cut through the subconscious without using LSD?

*Stephen:* Right.

*Interviewer:* So LSD was just a means?

*Stephen:* Right. Well, that's what it is. It's just pure energy and the energy raises your awareness, and then people you hear of who have hard trips, well, that's if someone has a lot of subconscious … if they have a lot of things they aren't admitting … a lot of things they have in their head that they aren't proud of … a lot of things that they've done that they don't think are good things to have done. The LSD will just like bring it right up in your face.

*Interviewer:* Is it in the form of colors and sounds?

*Stephen:* Well, it seems that you have a telepathic sense that corresponds with each physical sense, and you have ordinary vision, and then you have *clairvoyance*, which is French for clear vision. And you have ordinary hearing, and you have *clairaudience*, which is French for clear hearing. For touch you have compassion.

*Interviewer:* Realistically, Stephen ...

*Stephen:* Realistically!

*Interviewer:* How many of the others on Haight Street were able to do this genuinely and sincerely and how many were there for the fringe benefits?

*Stephen:* Well, in the beginning it was the majority could do it, and along toward the end it got into a lot of people who were like growing their hair and wearing the clothes and trying to talk the language but didn't know what it was that they were doing.

They imitated externals and didn't realize that the externals were superficial ... that the real thing was the mind thing. As far as how many people could do it, I've been in a rock hall in San Francisco when there was thirty-five hundred people in there that could do it.

*Interviewer:* Let me ask you this ... let me get back to a thing you said. You said you could communicate telepathically with someone if you are morally straight, or morally right. What is morally straight?

*Stephen:* Well, everybody knows that, really. Everybody knows what's straight. Everybody knows, never mind the word part, that if anybody's not really being straight with anybody the word part won't make a difference ... you know, the word part will be sort of void in the real action that's going on. Everybody knows if people are being good to people or not. Everybody knows where it's at.

*Interviewer:* That's too hard.

*Stephen:* What's too hard? Wait a minute, that's not too hard. Hang on for a minute. That's how it really is. Everybody really knows that. Then the thing is that you have to follow that. It's not just knowing that, like everybody knows that, but some folks follow it.

*Interviewer:* What is a moral person?

*Stephen:* Someone who is adult enough to make a contract with themselves that they can keep, who is not totally bent on their own ego. That would make a moral person, I think.

*Interviewer:* Is the Shakespearian phrase, "To thine own self be true" ... Is this a moral person, a person who is true to his own self no matter what his self tells him to be?

*Stephen:* I think there's a little place for elbow room in self-indulgence in there. I don't think that would do it. You do have to be true to yourself, but you have to be true to your best self, not to the self that wants to be heavier than other folks, or to the self that secretly thinks one is better than other people.

*Interviewer:* Is there any discipline in your moral person?

*Stephen:* Yeah, self-discipline. The only real discipline is self-discipline. If you can discipline yourself, other folks will accept your discipline, and if you can't discipline yourself, nobody will.

*Interviewer:* What is a spiritual person? We've been kicking around the term spiritual … what is a spiritual person?

*Stephen:* Well, the human existence is divided, according to ancient theology, Christian and whatnot, into three parts—the body, the soul, and the Spirit. The body is the material-plane part, and the soul is the region where all that telepathy and magic and all that stuff goes on. And the Spirit is pure God stuff—undifferentiated unity. So a spiritual person is one who is shooting for the top … who is trying to be spiritual rather than just magical or material.

*Interviewer:* Can you separate yourself … in your own mind?

*Stephen:* I don't separate it, I experience it like I experience my hands. Like as I touch one thing with my hands I can now touch with my soul. That's back to telepathy again. Telepathy is souls communicating like bodies can communicate.

*Interviewer:* What are you trying to teach? Is this what you're trying to teach, what you're telling me now and more?

*Stephen:* More, more. I'm trying to teach enlightenment. I'm a living American spiritual teacher, which is fairly rare.

*Interviewer:* Yeah, you don't find too many of them.

*Stephen:* What I really want to teach is enlightenment, and everything else is going to that.

*Interviewer:* But, you know, Stephen, every type of enlightenment always comes back to one thing, and that's your truth. There's a Baptist truth, there's a Jewish truth, there's a Catholic truth ….

*Stephen:* No, there's a previous truth to that.

*Interviewer:* How do you know?

*Stephen:* Because it's self-evident. A smile and a frown mean the same thing in any church.

*Interviewer:* Couldn't a smile be an expression of sadness sometimes?

*Stephen:* Oh, I suppose if a person wanted to do that and cross up the wiring, but the way monkeys generally do it is that they smile when it's a groove.

*Interviewer:* Okay, assuming that what you have is the way ...

*Stephen:* A way. Got to watch those very carefully.

*Interviewer:* There are many ways?

*Stephen:* Mm-hmm.

*Interviewer:* All right, let's take your way. First of all, the way a person should live ... how should a man live? Should he live as it is set up right now?

*Stephen:* Jesus said, "Love thy neighbor as thyself, and love thy God, and don't do what you hate, and don't lie," and that's about the basic ground rules that he put out for how to do it. Now if you could fit those basic ground rules down on top of how you're doing right now, then you're cool with what you're doing right now.

*Interviewer:* Now was he [Jesus] the best teacher?

*Stephen:* Best teacher is a funny thing.

*Interviewer:* Would he have it more than anybody else you've read about?

*Stephen:* No, I feel that Gautama Buddha and Jesus Christ are identical in fact.

*Interviewer:* They were one person?

*Stephen:* Their consciousness was one consciousness, although there were a couple of bodies separated by about five hundred years.

*Interviewer:* Who was the incarnation of whom?

*Stephen:* I think they're both incarnations of the same thing, which isn't anybody—it's everybody. That's the meaning of the Son of Man.

*Interviewer:* So Jesus never lived as a man?

*Stephen:* No, there was a carpenter named Jesus, who became the Christ, and there was a king's son named Gautama, who became a Buddha. Christ is a function word, not a name, and Christ was an avatar, which is to say a representative of God on earth. [An avatar is also what computer gamers call their character on the video screen.] An avatar is like ... you know, an oven has one little piece of itself that it sticks down inside the oven with a thermometer thing on the end of it to let the outside of the oven know what it's like inside.

And that's what the function of that kind of person is—to be right there in the oven of humanity—born, dying, pleasure, pain, whatever man is heir to. And how he does that affects the entire creation, because he's that link to the creation.

*Interviewer:* Did they say the same things, Jesus and Buddha? Were they identical in their philosophies?

*Stephen:* Yes, they did. They come in from different directions. They're identical as far as where they're going.

*Interviewer:* Stephen, are you able to tap into a source of energy ... you know, what do the Indians call it...?

*Stephen:* Kundalini.

*Interviewer:* Yeah. Are you able to tap into this?

*Stephen:* Yeah. I was into kundalini last night outrageous while I was at the Unitarian Church where we were talking, some of the best I've had for a while.

*Interviewer:* Well, you claim then that you can go back say two thousand years and tap into the conversation, to the energy ....

*Stephen:* No ... that's some more things. Kundalini is the life-force energy that a human being has that makes the difference whether you're crisp or wilted.

*Interviewer:* Yeah, yeah.

*Stephen:* And if you get a lot of it you get real crisp. You get very stoned. And if you don't get enough of it you get sick, and crazy, and you can get down where there's not very much of it, and you die. See, it's the life force.

*Interviewer:* Let me go on to something else. Human beings have a natural affinity to order, Stephen. They want order. I'm thinking of the order of the universe, the order of the planets and the stars, and so forth.

*Stephen:* There's some of that. But I think it's necessary to know that there's order and disorder, and that they're together. Like order defines disorder; disorder defines order. Yes defines no; no defines yes.

*Interviewer:* All right. Well anyway, tell me about your life. It's a disorderly life, as the establishment would have it.

*Stephen:* Oh boy.

*Interviewer:* Is that wrong?

*Stephen:* That's really wrong. Folks who think we're disorderly should try to come and travel with us and keep our discipline.

*Interviewer:* All right then. What is your life like in the bus, and with these people, and ....

*Stephen:* Well, life in the bus is the expediency of transportation to carry us out here around the United States to talk to everybody.

*Interviewer:* The bus is just a way.

*Stephen:* Right. But the thing about our life is that we be truthful with each other, even when it's hard to. There's a social difficulty to truth.

*Interviewer:* Why?

*Stephen:* Because a lot of folks don't want to be told where they're at.

*Interviewer:* But I mean what's so important about all this truth? As far as the spiritual truth, that's one thing, but as far as leveling with each other, why is that so important?

*Stephen:* Because you can't have one without the other. You have to be able to level with your fellow man before you can even hope to begin to try to level with the universe.

*Interviewer:* Is there ever any time that a variance of that truth between two people is more spiritual than the complete truth, in order to save someone's feelings?

*Stephen:* No, because feelings are an illusion. See, people who aren't telepathic think that their feelings are real. But if you get telepathic you realize that your feelings are phonemes and morphemes at a new level of semantics and communication.

*Interviewer:* Do you ever get angry?

*Stephen:* Not as much anymore. I used to. If I see anything approaching that looks like anger, I just try to cut loose of the whole thing … cut loose of everything. It's called non-attachment.

*Interviewer:* Is there a difference between detaching yourself and copping out?

*Stephen:* Oh yeah. If you see somebody's got their finger stuck in a light socket and they need you to help them out right now, you can have various alternatives of things to do. One of them is to freak out. One of them is to be compassionate, to reach over and do the right thing the first time. And it requires a measure of detachment to do the right thing the first time when it's heavy. That's why we be detached, so we don't let temporary ephemeral feelings affect heavy decisions.

Decisions should be made on principle, and on right, and on morals, not on the basis of emotions. You learn to be detached … so I don't deal in anger, I don't deal in fear, I don't deal in hate, and if people do those things to me, they can do those things to me if they want to and I won't do them back to them.

*Interviewer:* Is love an emotion?

*Stephen:* Love's the best one I recognize. It's like this: Love is pure energy, and other emotions flavor the energy.

*Interviewer:* Stephen, we talked about a lot of things, and I do appreciate your candor and your visit today. I thank you for talking with me.

*Stephen:* Thank you. I really enjoyed being here.

*Q: Do you believe in evolution?*

Sure. I think we're all evolving. Do you mean specifically the kind they talked about in the Scopes trial?

*Q: … Uh-huh.*

Yes, I really do. I can see it's so obvious and so self-evident you know, you can just look. There was a man who came into my bus one time, and he had a little monkey. I have a horn I blow sometimes … cow horn. I use it like they use a shofar in the Jewish Church. And I blew the horn, and she was really intrigued with it. It's the kind where you've got to go *Ppe-e-w-w-w* to make it work, and she was going *Ssh-h-e-e-o-o-u-u-u* … whew, and she couldn't get it to do anything. I reached over and I went *Pptth-pptth*, like that at her the way you do with a trumpet. And when I did, she dropped the horn and threw both arms around my neck and started kissing me on the ear and gibbering at me and pulling on my hair and messing with me, because she was delighted at the communication. Because I'd been down home with her and tried to talk to her and hadn't come on with an ego trip because I was Homo sapiens ….

There sure are a lot of beatniks in these buses. Besides talking about the route and the way we're going to go, there's a bunch of other stuff we got to do ... which is, I don't know how it came about, maybe we just got soft and sloppy from having such a nice place to park for five days, but we was a really sloppy group head on the road yesterday.

For instance, when I pulled in here last night I pulled over to the extreme right until I almost had one wheel hanging over into the grass all the way around, hoping that the bus behind me would do that and the one behind them would do that so that when we came all the way around here and stopped, the first row of buses would be as far out as possible so there'd be enough room left for everybody else. I came back on the grass and the bus behind me was six feet back from the grass and the one behind him was way back in the middle of the street.

We had to do all that see-sawing and backing up because nobody paid attention coming in. You could have figured it out for yourself, I didn't have to think of that. There's something about being telepathic ... you know, where's that at? Then there's that business about when we cross an intersection and the light changes and somebody's afraid they're going to get left behind at the light, so they pull out in the middle of a yellow light and get stopped in the middle of the intersection and block all the traffic going both ways until the light changes, because they aren't paying enough attention.

They have their eyes fixed on the mandala in front like an elephant with their nose wrapped around the tail of the elephant in front. Sometimes I feel like I'm the only person on the Caravan driving, like I'm driving and everybody else is just hanging on and following the string. I can drive the first fifteen or twenty vehicles pretty good, but the ones I can't see back a couple of miles, it's hard to drive for them. They got to take a little initiative and drive for themselves.

Also every bus on this Caravan is responsible for every other bus on the Caravan, and if you see that the man in front of you is stretching out so far and the man behind you is stretching out so far that there's danger of losing contact, you're supposed to take the responsibility on yourself to do something about it ... whatever is appropriate at the time, if you have to blow a green light to be sure that you don't lose contact with the rest of them.

If you know who made the turn in front and you see they went out of sight, then you have to maybe hang up for a while because you're the link to the Caravan, because if you go and run through that light and the man behind you didn't see that turn get made ... we break the Caravan up like that. That isn't being compassionate with each other, it isn't being telepathic, it isn't being one thing.

About parking ... this is a public parking place. For all we know a Silver Stream convoy might come in right after us and want to be here too, and we ought to give them room if we can. We ought to be economical. Wasting space like that is like wasting food, it's not any different. It's wasting something. It's making it harder for somebody else to get some of it.

That means everybody's got to keep their wits about them at that place and always remember that we're a whole thing and each person is responsible for the whole thing. If we move and each one is taking responsibility for himself, we're no burden on anybody, but if we got to drag through ... like in Paducah.

It was fun having a police escort through Paducah, but the major reason we had a police escort through Paducah was because we scared them so bad trying to get out of that filling station. Because we got out and blocked all the traffic and all that, and they figured that they'd rather stop all the red lights in town until they got rid of us, because they were afraid that we weren't smart enough to get through their town without blowing it. That's why they gave us a police escort. You know that?

We can't have buses sticking out into the interstate. There were buses sticking halfway out into a lane of traffic. It's better to go on by and pull off ahead of the Caravan, even if it's five miles, than to stop with your tail end sticking out into the traffic like that.

How are we fixed for gasoline? Does anybody need gasoline right away? Why don't the folks that need gasoline right away just pick up right now and go get it and pick us up along the way. Everybody else, we're going to pull out in about ten minutes. Like stow and go. We're going to make a Caravan gas stop in about thirty or forty miles any-way. Okay?

*Along toward the last of the tour there were a couple of places where I spoke that I don't remember very well because I'd been on the road so long, I was so tired and so sleepy that it was extremely difficult to sit on stage and make sense, and especially to look out and see the Farm folks dozing in the front row. Most of the time, we had a good time with 'em, we got 'em off, they loved us, we carried the word around the United States that peace is possible and we were peaceful, you didn't have to be vio-lent, warlike, and dangerous to be for peace, that the way to be for peace is by being peaceful about being for peace. That was honored, and we were taken care of quite well by the United States while we were out.*

*Q: Could you rap about music? I don't mean popular music, I mean music as a yoga.*

The OM we were all singing together—that's music as a yoga, some of it, making everything, every sound thing you do, be music. Tuning your motor so it runs right is being a musician. There's a way when it sounds good and a way when it doesn't sound good … a way when it's harmonious. Music is the expression of harmony in sound; love is the expression of harmony in life. And if you express harmony it helps out the whole system. If you make harmony it makes a gestalt medium in which other things which may have been disharmonious before can be integrated and also become harmonious. By every harmony you create, you create more harmonies. Harmonies have holes in them where other people can put their harmony in, too. And that's what music is about is harmony. Harmony is what allows there to be lots of different ways and lots of different individualities but all heavy in one thing.

*Q: Is truth relative or absolute?*

Truth is absolute. Relative truth is relative. The Fourteenth Dalai Lama said, "There's two kinds of truth—relative truth, absolute truth. Relative truth deals with knowledge. Absolute truth deals with wisdom." Seldom is a yardstick exactly thirty-six inches long. But the idea of a thirty-six-inch yardstick is still an absolute. And they've probably dropped off a few perfect thirty-six-inch ones out of the place where they make the wooden yardsticks. There's probably been a few perfect ones drop out and they never knew the difference ….

 hat's really important to start off with at the beginning is that there is Spirit, and there is man, and there is communion. And people still have communion, and this is communion. And we came to have communion with you. That's why the Caravan came out from San Francisco across the country was to come out and have communion. We found out that there is a way for people to fit together that makes it so a lot of them can be together and cooperate and be happy

Now the kind of education I had said that religion wasn't even real … not that any particular one wasn't or anything like that, but that none of them were … that it was something nobody very heavy had anything to do with. You've heard, "Get into computer programming, that's where the brains are going this season." Well, this season the brains are going into programming their own minds. And it's going to make a great difference. And when I say mind I mean something that is supposed to be encompassing, so as to exclude no one.

Now I think that for me the most exciting way for that to come out is for us to do questions and answers, and pick it out piece by piece and see what do we really want to know. We can get the same information that way as if I talked for half an hour, except I think it gets us higher. So let's just start right off. Give me somebody to talk to. Got a hand back there.

*[Q: unintelligible]*   Right. He says when I'm talking about a way that includes everybody, does it include unintelligent people or blind people or deaf people or people who can't understand a very sophisticated thing.

Yes. At its nitty-gritty, religion is supposed to be nonverbal. A couple of monkeys are supposed to be able to look at each other and know that each other's cool. And if you can't, somebody's faking it. Now if that makes ninety-nine per cent of your relationships weird, maybe you've got to straighten up. A person can have several senses not working and you can still communicate with them if you're compassionate, because compassion cuts through all that other stuff. A person doesn't have to be smart to know a kind touch. So compassion covers that kind of thing.

There may be people who may not want to learn certain disciplines to get themselves as high as they can get. What you do about those folks, what a religion does about those folks is that it stays compassionate with them. And you can learn to carry your share and then some more.

It doesn't take too much work to keep one person high. From one end of the scale they start off and say, "Wow, if you get stoned, far out, whew, wouldn't that be neat."

On the other hand, it's not from that end of the scale you're supposed to be looking at it. You're supposed to be saying, "Yes, I can get stoned, and I can stone everybody I run into all day long, too." Supposed to be putting out juice, not taking it in.

And if you're putting it out then it covers those folks, and as far as unintelligent people goes, there isn't any such thing as unintelligent folks, there's only unintelligent situations. I don't believe in folks being smarter or dumber than one another. I think if somebody in a hassle says that the other fellow's dumb, they're both in a dumb trip. It's dumb astral weather. Because we're all in the same trip, whatever it is.

*Q: Why are you the one out of the Caravan always leading the conversation if we're all on the same trip?*

Well, first, I was the one who was asked to go on the speaking tour. The Caravan happened as a result of that. I think that we have been discussing that question in San Francisco for about five years, and here's the way the class works. It's open doors and it's free and everybody can come in, and the way it's always been is that the questions I like best are the ones that start with "what about" and "what if."

*Q: Would you explain what you meant about the communion?*

Everybody was having a common purpose when we got here, and pretty much a centered focus, too. There was a pretty good level of meditation happening before I even got here, because everybody was waiting for the same thing. Then when I started with the horn and attracted people's attention to the central focus on a plane and everybody started OMing, we made something happen that was so loud and so strong and so vibrationally heavy that there was nothing else you could pay attention to.

*Q: So then the communion thing was everyone doing something together.*

Well, no, this is still going toward it. Now when the OMing and the horn-blowing all stopped, then we were there, and what we were was a pure telepathic medium with no messages in it yet. That's communion. So as long as we're still putting messages in it, it's a kind of communion, but pure communion is no messages. It's to come here and know that we're really one.

*Q: When you were speaking of communion you said there is a God.*

Right. I should be more specific. I did not say "a" God. For me the whole universe is god from the newest baby to the oldest galaxy. There isn't anything else that is omnipotent, omnipresent, and omniscient. All power all knowledge and everywhere at once? Only the complete universal, total, manifestation fills the bill.

*Q: ... How do you know? Is there a pre-enlightened rational argument that demonstrates this?*

As the fellows who wrote the Declaration of Independence said, "we hold these truths to be self evident." The "All" may not be apprehended through Aristotelian logic.

*Q: ... Is there a way?*

Yes. By direct revelation, by direct knowledge. It is not given to us to figure it out, because that would make us able to comprehend the All. Well, comprehending the All would make you bigger than the All. Can't do it because the All is everything. Can't be bigger than everything. But you can experience oneness with it and be everything. And you can know it by direct cognition. But you can't figure it out by Aristotelian logic. And when you do know it, you can see there's nothing contradictory.

*Q: Are psychedelics the only way?*

No, you can go by many paths. I don't come out and say that psychedelics are the path, I just say psychedelics are a path. Don't let anybody say that it isn't one of them. But the classical enlightenment path is schizophrenia, and the question is, would I recommend that for everybody? Schizophrenia is when you get so crazy that it's a place where, "When you're in the dark night of the soul, call on me." And if you do that, it's just the same thing as flipping a bad trip to a good trip. You can go from full-blown schizophrenia to enlightenment, if you have faith at the nitty-gritty place.

*[Q: unintelligible]*   Religion in general is groups of folks. Now I think that when we were in the place that I called a communion earlier, I don't think there was anybody here who was not enlightened at that time. Does everybody understand that? What else were we doing? We were being cool right here in the here and now. Everybody's head was at peace. Everybody was focused on a single thing. Everybody was cool.

Don't think of enlightenment as you go along this road for years and years and years and years and then there's a great big golden gate and you go in and they put a thing around your neck and say, "Zap, you're enlightened!" It's that every once in a while you have flashes of sanity and they get closer together, till pretty soon you got a straight string of it and you say, "Far out, this is it."

*Q: Can you be more specific about enlightenment and schizophrenia?*

What they call schizophrenia is getting so spaced that you start getting into the astral plane. And you start getting into, quote, hallucinations. That's one of the symptoms of insanity, classically, is hallucinations. Well, that's one of the symptoms of being stoned, too. And there's no such thing as hallucinations. You just see what's there at another level.

But it's there. It's not not there. Maybe you're making it be there, but it's there because you're making it be there then. And it's there for everybody who has a viewer. Somebody who gets really schizophrenic can get into that place where schizophrenia isn't by itself, it's with paranoia. Now paranoia and schizophrenia go together, and they're both ego.

Schizophrenia is following paranoia so far to protect your ego that you forgot where you started. But once you're spaced and on that trip, if you just say, "Wow, everything around me is fluid and wild and it's reacting to my thoughts as fast as I can think, the only thing I can do is get straight." If you're in this culture you go for Jesus. If you're a Buddhist you go for Buddha. But you get to that place where you say, "Wow, man, if that's happening, if everything I think is making a difference, I can't do anything but get straight."

And I can talk to schizophrenics really well because sometimes we're seeing the same stuff. They've got third eye. Schizophrenics and babies are neat to talk to.

*Q: You said before that you have already reached enlightenment ...*

Already. I don't like already.

*Q: … Have you?*

There's a process, and the enlightened man can think an ordinary thought and be ordinary, and the ordinary man can think an enlightened thought and be enlightened. And if you're cool, you think a lot of enlightened thoughts in a row and they stay pretty good that way. It's a process thing. I don't like to think of it as now you are, now you aren't. That depends on your contract with yourself. I made a contract with myself about a way I was going to be the rest of my life, and I try not to break that contract.

*Q: What do you mean by the Christ?*

Christ is the name of a function and Buddha is the name of a function that is served for all of mankind. It's the function of a redeemer. Christ was a redeemer … Christ is a redeemer. To know what a redeemer is you've got to know what a deemer is. And a deemer is one who deems. To deem is to estimate or to make a judgment and say, "I think that's about fair." And if somebody else has made a judgment about that and you come along and you look at it and say, "I think that's about fair," you redeem it. You put value into it, you assign it its value.

Well, the redeemer assigns the value to the entire system. And the system sometimes gets funky all over. All of creation gets like a room with the windows all closed and gets stuffy. A redeemer lets a little fresh air through … just by going through and looking at everything, experiencing everything, and saying, "That's heavy, that's real … that thirty-six inches must be a yard." And he goes through making his estimates, because the redeemer is supposed to have a perfect eye to judge with.

Like the Inspector General comes through now and then and he says, "There it is, it's the one that's cool, that's the one that works … that one's got to shape up, that one's okay …." The way you be shows how much value you put into things. How you talk isn't so important as how you be.

*Q: What is death?*

Death is when this piece of the organism terminates its contract, when you wear out your biological machine so it doesn't work anymore, when your memory banks are so clogged up it's time to junk that memory bank and get a new one. It's okay. You're born and you die, it's a contract. Like credit and debit, it comes out even. Everybody's born and everybody dies, that's cool. It's a privilege to get to be here at all. First breath is a blessing.

*[Q: unintelligible]* I'm a spiritual teacher. As a spiritual teacher, talking is a hobby with me. Talking isn't really where it's at. That isn't really what I do the most of or even what I do best. I do other things. It's hard for me to talk in this area just because it's this area. But I can help people be better who want to be better because I want them to be better, too. I can look at somebody who isn't in very good shape and want them to be in better shape and help them get in better shape. That isn't magic, it's communication.

*Q: I saw you up at Grinnell, and I got the impression at the time that you advocated acid as the best way to achieve enlightenment.*

No, that must have been a misapprehension. I've only taken acid once in the last year and I was dosed then. It got me high and I got high enough to look around and get selective, and when I was at the peak of it, just as stoned as I could get, off the wheel of life, understanding the entire trip, all that place, I got a little message and it said, "Courtesy of acid intelligence: You aren't gonna take any more acid." I said, "All right."

*Q: ... Then you definitely feel that there's other ways to achieve good karma without drugs?*

Sure. But I still think that peyote is good used in ceremony or in other places, too. I think that grass really helps us a lot ... that psychedelics can be used to help out the whole thing. But if you're going to go for broke for enlightenment you better love the truth. Because if I hadn't loved truth, acid wouldn't have got me high.

I feel like I want to cut loose here. I love you all, and thank you for coming here. You'll be hearing more from us because we aren't going to quit doing what we're doing. I hope you don't either, and God Bless you and thank you and good night.

Caravan! We're going to go out to the highway out 70 to the rest stop by Booneville. We don't even have to go out by caravan. Let's just meet out by the rest stop by Booneville.

*Q: How far is Booneville?*

It's only about twenty miles past where we were. Okay? Anyone can caravan with me who wants to. Just truck on out.

**W**e're here in a church building, and this is all put together to do a church ritual. Here's how you have a ritual: When a bunch of people get together they have to discuss and decide among them what are the ground rules for that get-together so they know what kind of a deal they're putting their energy into. If you have a whole lot of gatherings of people and you ask those same questions and get those same answers about those things, if you do it long enough it gets to be a ritual.

I feel like that's kind of preparatory to us having a conversation. We started out from San Francisco and we've been all over the place, talked to a whole lot of folks. We know what the country's like because we've just been through it, and we want to talk with you here. Somebody about fifty, sixty feet back ask a question so I can reach back there.

*Q: Who are you and where are you going?*

My name is Stephen. I was born in Colorado. Where are we going is we're going to keep right on doing this. By this I mean trying to get folks together, at any level. Right now we're going to leave here tonight and go on to Tulsa, Oklahoma. We're going from Tulsa to Boulder, Colorado, then New Mexico and Los Angeles, and then San Francisco, which may be the heaviest thing on the trip. We've been gone a long time and we've changed a lot. It may be far out when we get back. We've really learned a lot on the road.

*Q: What about going back to the land?*

Well, I'm not in the commune marriage broker business or anything, but I feel that I know a whole bunch of folks that want to live together and try to do a thing. I'm going to have as many of them live with me as can live on one piece of land, and then if we have more than that, we're going to have to get into more farms. If we do that, if somebody really wants to do a community-agricultural thing along our lines, we'll come and hang out with them a couple of months and try to help them get it started.

*Q: How can we keep in communication with you?*

I think that we'll always be easily found. When we get back to San Francisco we'll be there for a while, and then after that we'll be looking for a farm and I think the way will be marked because we're going to travel together.

*Q: What can each one of us do to help alleviate the suffering of the world?*

That's a good question. The first thing is that you be aware of it and recognize it unsentimentally … that you just be really aware of what it's like. Then the next thing you do is you don't be bummed by it, because that makes you contribute to it.

What you do is you take care of the first thing at hand, which is right between your ears. Fix your head. When you fix your head folks will notice, and if you just be honest and down home and communicate with folks about where you're at, you'll transmit your magic to them. If your head feels okay, take the next problem in front of you and work on that.

*Q: … Is that about total responsibility?*

Total responsibility … right, that if you look out and you don't like the shape of the world, go inside and start cleaning house and it'll get better out there. Then, don't be afraid to work hard in the material plane, too.

*Q: How do you fix your head?*

You have to tell the truth all the time even in uncomfortable situations, even if there's great social difficulty. What that does is it keeps you from having subconscious, and if you don't have subconscious you should be smart enough to figure everything else out yourself.

If you don't have subconscious, the clear light can shine through you. Your own subconscious is the filter that keeps that out. Then if you come to a perfectly square realization that you're karmically clean with everybody you meet, your cause and effect is cool. What that means is you have to be groovy for a long time, until you can say, "I can look back down my chain and I know what I've been doing and I now have knowledge of good karma." If you have knowledge of good karma, then you can come on pretty heavy behind it. That's what moral force is. It doesn't mean going limp when the cops pick you up. It means knowing where you're at, so you're strong.

*Q: When you look at the world unsentimentally, as you said, what do you see?*

It looks to me, upon going out and seeing it first hand, a lot better than the media made me think it was. For a while I was believing the media and thinking it was really bad off, but it's not that way, because the media multiplies the hassles by thousands and thousands of times. What we find going out on the road and really being with people is that we have very few hassles.

*Q: I feel that very recently I've made a decision to get straight, but before that I put a lot of bad vibrations on people. Do I need to be concerned about that as well as trying to be pure?*

Here's the thing, if you've been hassling your friends or your family and then you decide you have to straighten up, then you really do have to go to each one of them that you had a hassle with and get straight with them. Straight with them is when you feel right with them, not when you give them a present or anything like that, but when you feel straight with them. You have to go get that way with each one of them, and that cancels all the bad vibrations that you put into those folks, because we have the power of forgiveness, which is a heavy power. By forgiveness you can take the evil out of bad deeds.

*Q: Does forgiveness imply blame?*

No. Forgiveness is another kind of a thing. If somebody came along and took your thing, and then later on down the line they got caught and somebody says, "Hey, I caught this fellow that took your thing, what should I do to him?" and you think, Wow, I don't want to do anything to him, what you can say is, "I give it to him now, retroactively. I fore-give him." Isn't that neat? You say, "It's okay, you could have had my permission to do that. It's cool."

*Q: If you know you've given someone pain, how do you handle it?*

The first thing you do is you don't do it anymore.

*Q: ... I mean if you've already done it.*

If you've already done it, then what you have to do is straighten up and groove in the here and now—same instructions all the time. As soon as you get done doing something dumb, straighten up and groove in the here and now. That's how you can get it back. You have to learn to forgive yourself at a place like that and say, "Okay." It's not that you can't blow it—free will implies that you can blow it. The heavy thing is that you can always get it back.

*Q: What is God's will for man?*

God's will for man is free will and a fair shake, and then the rest is man's part. You start off and then you make your own thing from what you have been given. From there you can merge with the universe by seeing that you can decide that you'll be like the universe and give everybody a fair shake, too.

*Q: I've been wondering if the work you do now as a teacher is different from the work you did before as a teacher. I'm sitting here thinking that it must be easier now than it was.*

It's two ways about that—it's easier for me because I never have to wonder what I'm going to say, because the truth's the first thing on the top of my head. I'm just committed to truth. Now before, I used to teach people things where I had a curriculum or something to teach them, and any human contact we did was on the side. They said that you were an interesting teacher if you also made human contact while you did the information thing. Well, I found out the information thing was a shuck, and I didn't want to do it. I would rather do the people thing.

*Q: I still see similarities in your work and things like my husband and I do.* What do you do?

*Q: ... This church.*

Ah-ha. Thank you for letting us be in your church.

*Q: ... And I feel a little jealous of the way you're doing it.*

Jealous of the way I'm doing it—I don't understand.

*Q: I would give anything to hear you here on Sunday mornings and see how you could tackle this group here—half-filled pews on Sunday mornings. This is what I'm talking about being hard, compared to this right now tonight. This is almost like a happening, like a celebration in itself.*

Yes. On the other hand, I had to drive seven thousand miles to get here. Lots of adventures happened to us on the way, and it was a groove, and it was all for the glory of the thing, but we've been through some changes.

And this is a pretty big room; you're doing good to get it half full. When I started doing a thing like this, for the first six months I was doing it, I started with twelve people and ended up with six. The first night I had a meeting I got into such a hassle with some fellow it broke up the meeting.

This work is the same work that your husband's doing, that's what they do here in these places. He does it too, and I'm really glad. If you're doing the work it doesn't matter about uniforms or wages or fringe benefits or insurance or any of that. It's all for the same company anyway.

*Q: How do you keep building faith in yourself not to do other people wrong?*

That's really a good thing to do. The way you do it is that when you're in a situation with somebody you have to remember to stop and pay attention and be sure you're being fair with them. After you do that for a while it becomes your habit to do that. After you've done that for a long while, you get to where you can trust yourself. They say in Tibetan yoga, "Where there's lack of faith there's lack of good faith." Confidence means with-faithness. If your faith is good then you'll be strong in the knowledge of it, and you'll have confidence to move with. It comes from the long haul.

*Q: Could the criterion for just being straight be as simple as merely not making that person uptight?*

Not quite. You ought to gas them some, too. The way you ought to be with other people is you have to not only not put them uptight but you ought to spot them a little extra energy to help them get on with. If you put it out, it'll come back. If you say you're going to hang on to it, that's the off button. You don't care that it comes back, but it does come back.

I think I'd like to let us go here because we really all know where it's at. I was really glad to get to be here. Thanks to your husband for that.

God Bless you all, and thank you all for coming and being here. Good night and God Bless you.

---

*As the Caravan came through Oklahoma, coming up to Tulsa, we were given a place to park that was kind of a big outdoor park. I think there were even swings in it, but it had enough places we could get the Caravan off the road and stop for a while. And we weren't parked really close to anybody else at the time, when somebody came and banged on the front door.*

*And Michael, I thought rashly—it was a school bus and he had the handle, he could open it or not—he opened the door for them. Two men stepped up into the stepwell. And one said to the other, "You got your pocket knife,*

Lukey? These people need a haircut." And Michael, in what was the bravest thing I ever saw him do, dived from the driver's seat and knocked them out the door with his body. And I pulled the door shut until I saw I had to move over and jump out, too, and gave a shout to Ina May to be ready to pop the handle across, and I jumped out and pushed it shut.

One guy, who swung on Michael, had his belt wrapped around his hand and had about ten inches of belt sticking out of his hand and the buckle. And he hit Michael in the head with that, edgeways, so hard that the buckle cut off a swath of hair against his skull. And I kicked that guy.

And then everything came to a stop. It was like I knew right then at that moment that I could make this fight go on or I could stop this fight right now. And I knew what I had to do. I called Michael, and we got back on the bus.

After we got them out of the bus, they knocked out all of the windows down one side, which was next to the kids' beds. They were walking around on the roof of the bus and jumping on the hood, four or five of them, something like that.

And so we didn't pull out in the morning. We took another day. Our bus was made by the Gillig Bus Company, and everybody on the Caravan who had a Gillig donated a window and fixed us up spiff and new, looked like nothing ever happened to us.

here's really such a lot of power in Sunday morning. It feels so good, really good to come stand with you and be quiet for a while. Sometimes we have to go so fast for so long that we hardly ever get to slow down and notice what it is we're doing. I can remember real good when it's like this. We're going to have a stream of folks out here all day today.

They put us on the TV last night and told where we were and said we were holding a meeting today. So like we're going to have lots of opportunities to be wise. Take care of what bus business you need to today, but don't take care of anything you don't need to. Try to spend some time today hanging out and being easy and being gentle and letting your head out because we've been running hard for a few days. If we're going to help out Tulsa and all that, we've got to be gentle and soft. God Bless you. I'll see you later on during the day. Thank you for coming out and being with me this morning.

*Interviewer:* They go loosely by the name of Monday Night Class, and they're led by a San Francisco minister who not so many months ago was teaching every Monday night to a large group of San Franciscans, who like himself and like the members of this traveling version want to share their religious experience with the world, or at least that part of the world accessible by bus.

*Stephen:* The folks in the Caravan just asked to come along with me. I never asked to have a Caravan and it just sort of floated up. And once it's here, well then I have to take care of it because it's the first immediate thing around me and that's the thing I have to take care of. But I don't have to do much taking care of, because the folks didn't come for me to take care of them.

They came to help me, and so they take care of themselves, they take care of their hassles, they take care of their food, and they not only take care of themselves, they take care of me at a material level. Something happens to my bus, I have people come and help me fix it right away and keep it together, and everybody just sort of cooperates on getting all of us where we go.

*Interviewer:* When you talk to Stephen and other members of the Caravan you soon discover that theirs is a religion of camaraderie and trust.

*Stephen:* We're prepared to absorb anything in order to communicate and re-establish a bond of trust. We want to come right out and be with folks.

*Interviewer [speaking to girl in Caravan]:* Do you like traveling around like this or would you rather be in one place, settle down?

*Girl:* I really dig traveling around, but I also dig settling down—whatever I'm doing I'm digging. We're planning to settle down on a farm after this, and that'll be really settling down.

*Interviewer:* You don't know where it'll be.

*Girl:* No. We haven't decided yet. We've seen good places in Georgia, good places in Oregon, California. Wherever it is, we've seen good country all over the country.

*Stephen:* Funny thing about coming to Oklahoma; my great-grandfather was a U.S. Marshal in the Oklahoma Indian Territory, and I have an aunt living now who was born in the Oklahoma Indian Territory when it was still territory, so I don't feel very alienated down here a bit. It feels like some place I've been before.

*Interviewer:* Over the past few months the Caravan has covered most of the United States. All in all, the group has been accepted, and occasionally they have been encouraged to hold public services along the way. There was even time for them to pause and deliver six new infant arrivals into the Caravan, all by natural birth, and all within the bounds of matrimony.

*Stephen:* We have people who are single folks, we have people who are married folks, and we keep our marriage contracts, and they're lifetime, and we take care of our kids and we know who's the daddy and all that kind of thing. Some folks think I'm strict. I say if you're making love you're engaged, and if you're pregnant you're married.

*Interviewer:* The next stop for the Caravan will be in Boulder, Colorado. They will stop for a while, meet as many people as possible, and then continue their journey on to San Francisco. There the group will park their buses and eventually take up living off the land, but the imprints left behind by the tires on the buses and the thoughts and the minds of the Monday Night Class will always be there.

Two hundred and fifty people are traveling with this Caravan; all ages are represented, and the travelers come from all walks of life. Many have college degrees and many were once professional people who left high-paying jobs. They have been on the road for three and a half months and have traveled eight thousand miles. The group's leader, called simply Stephen, says they will be in Tulsa three days and will then head for Boulder, Colorado. When Stephen left San Francisco for a speaking tour his students followed.

*Stephen:* I've been teaching in San Francisco about five years and for the last couple of years I've had about fifteen hundred people every Monday night. We've been teaching a peaceful way and been having some progress in spiritual development and so I got invited out to speak across the country. When I told the class I was going to have to recess class to go out and talk, a lot of them said, "Can we go?"

*Interviewer:* How about acceptance? How well are you accepted, say with city officials or with the traffic police, highway patrol, state police?

*Stephen:* We found out that if you really want to see a cop spring to attention you ask him for help. And when we've needed help we've just been open and asked for it, called the sheriff and said, "Hey, our parking space fell through, we need a place to park." And they fixed us up in Minnesota with a Boy Scout camp and somewhere else with a state park. Had the Director of Natural Resources in Rhode Island give us the nicest park in New England to stay in, and he came under political fire for doing it, and he said beautiful things about how these people are like the old pioneers and it's just like when Roger Williams got kicked out of Boston and came down to start Providence and all that.

I was reading Genesis the other day, and I found out they always say that God wasted the world in the flood and all that business because folks was fornicating and doing all that kind of thing, and in Genesis it says he wasted them for violence. Right in the front of it, it says that's what they flooded the world for was for violence, specifically.

*Interviewer:* Do you think the Bible is taken out of context quite a bit?

*Stephen:* Oh sure, but it's a heavy Holy Book, and people have forgotten what it is—it's the logbook for the last few thousand years that we're keeping here. All the monkeys have got to keep a logbook to find out what happened on the planet.

*Interviewer:* When Horace Greeley wrote, "Go west, young man," over one hundred years ago, he was advising the young people of his day to go west to seek the happiness of fame and fortune. These young people don't seem to be on a journey for fame and fortune. Perhaps they possess enough happiness without it.

The Continental Divide's down there. We should be able to start seeing the mountains in about a hundred and fifty miles. So we may be able to see them by sundown. We're kind of like on a little north leg right now and we're going to bend over more westerly pretty quick. Okay, ready to do it? Alrighty, let's do it.

*This transcript was strangely lost, but we give you the story of what happened to us on the way to the gig.*

*Colorado was an adventure all its own. We were all parked up above Boulder in somebody's big farm field. Pretty soon this guy came up, and he was obviously spooked and scared, and he was saying, "They're coming to get you! They're coming to get you! They've got horses and dogs and ropes and guns and pickups. They're coming to get you!"*

*He was afraid! He was afraid. And I thought, Well, I know what to do about this. And I went out and got the buses and said, "Stow and go, stow and go, we're leaving immediately." And the bus people had good discipline. They loaded right up and they got those buses ready, and we started pulling out of the field and onto the highway and heading for Boulder. And just as we left, I told somebody who had a car, "You go on into Boulder to the police station and tell 'em that I'm going to come and park the Caravan in the police station parking lot."*

*As we left the field, there was a pickup truck full of drunk cowboys, and then a school bus full of hippies, and then another pickup truck full of drunk cowboys and another school bus full of hippies and another pickup truck full of drunk cowboys. And we went toward Boulder like that, and when we got there, at the first intersection outside of Boulder, there was a mess of cops, sheriffs, deputies. And I got out and told them my plan was to go to the police parking lot and park.*

*They said, "You don't have to do that. You can go on back to that field and park right there."*

*"I said, "How about all of those cowboys?"*

*He said, "My deputies will be at your gate, and those cowboys will stay away."*

*And then he told us, who were in the first bus, "You make a U-turn, just head on back."*

And I made my U-turn, and as I made my U-turn, he told the pickup truck behind me to go straight, school bus U-turn, pickup truck go straight, till we were all sorted out from the cowboys, back down to our field, and socked in for the night. I told 'em in the drivers' meeting in the field just before we left to go out that a school bus in lowest granny gear could push a pickup truck with its brakes locked, indefinitely, so we were prepared for whatever came.

The other thing that was the end of that story was when I did my gig in Boulder, I took time to do a little gratuitous hassle on the cowboys and talked about these guys that got all their sadistic leather and guns trip, and they're all like flamenco guys with a rose in their teeth and a thorn in their lip, and they weren't really a real brave bunch of guys to come down all liquored up and well-armed to take on a bunch of hippies. That's how people get when they get drunk sometimes.

Maybe we should flee on to California. What does anybody think about that? Just fly on to the coast? Whew ... yeah, I guess everybody does think that, huh? Well look then, we'll go on down the road a ways and the Santa Fe police will pick us up outside Santa Fe, and when they do they'll guide us to a gas stop.

*When the New Mexico police came up, they were in the old-fashioned New Mexico police costumes with the cloth hat with the shiny black visor, and they were all Mexican, I noticed. And they checked us out enough to notice that I didn't have a driver's license.*

*About that time another car came up. It was an old Anglo sheriff with his pistol rig hung down low on his hip and his big cowboy hat. And he came over to us and said, "What's your plan?"*

*I said, "I'm going to drive on out, back to California."*

*He said, "How long you think it'll be taking you?"*

*"Oh, it won't take us very much time at all. The only thing hanging us up right now, in fact, is that highway patrol trooper over there wants to write me a ticket for not having a driver's license."*

*And the old sheriff says, "Well, I'll tell you what. Don't you worry about a thing. I'll take care of him, and you guys can just take right on off."*

*I said, "Well, thank you." And we both knew that we were both doing what we both wanted, although we probably didn't have that close of a friendly relationship between us. But we did what the sheriff said and we were gone.*

*Q: And what was the purpose of the trip?*

The purpose of the trip was to go out and put the word on folks.

When the Caravan got back into San Francisco, we'd come across off the Bay Freeway and onto Montgomery Street, the heart of the financial district. And as we cruised down Montgomery Street, we were hanging out the windows and waving at people and throwing 'em books and posters.

Suddenly the cops came out and stopped us all, and this cop who I knew came out and looked at us and he says, to the other cops, "I know who these guys are. They're okay. Let them pass."

The cop who said that was the one that I'd talked to when there'd been a bomb set near the Park Street police station. We felt real bad about that. We didn't feel that represented our head at all. And I'd gone to the Park Street police station and said, "I know thousands and thousands of hippies who are really sorry that anybody would ever do a thing like that to you."

And that was the guy that came down, when we were the biggest, noisiest, most outrageous thing that had ever landed on Montgomery Street in the history of San Francisco, and he was the guy who stepped forward and said to the other cops, "These guys are okay. I don't need any backup."

We've been talking in San Francisco for almost five years this month about one thing or another. I've talked about all kinds of religions and psychologies and universal models and ways your head works. But the thing that I talked about that was mostly the thing that I learned myself from my own experience was about how attention works.

Attention is energy, just like $E=mc^2$, an equation that works straight across just like that. And each one of you can have control over your attention. A lot of you don't, as we noticed by the dogs and babies this morning. That'd get heavy now and then. That's when they could attract enough people's heads to have enough juice to be heavy in the manifestation for a while.

So here's the way it works about attention: Whatever you put your attention on you get more of. Whatever you put your attention on you amplify and make that thing stronger and more so in the world. And I've been teaching that in San Francisco for about five years. This trip we took out across the country, like all good trips, expanded our consciousness.

I've been saying that about attention so long that I believe it myself now. Therefore I can't put my attention into a city scene anymore. Because the worst thing happening on the planet is the cities. Like the cities are the major cause of warfare, poverty, totalitarian police state, whatnot.

All those things are functions of being crowded up in cities. One time a year or so ago, maybe a couple of years, I got into an outrageous trip on Mount Tamalpais—got very stoned, got a real good look at the nature scene, talked to some trees. When I went back down to my house and looked at what was on the walls, I saw that we had a whole mess of arty but violent crap on the walls.

That was weird stuff for us to be putting our head in. And we had to clean off the walls to just leave only stuff that we wanted to manifest more of by looking at—not something just because it was interesting or cute or strange or bizarre. That's manifesting an eye in the place of an eye and a hand in the place of a hand. Now all this stuff is alive. You and me and the ground and the sky and the dogs and the foghorns, concrete retaining wall, is all alive, and it all has a soul, and its soul can be communicated with, enhanced or depressed, by the human beings in the area. All this stuff is alive and if you interact with it it'll take care of you.

So today is kind of a Caravan drivers' meeting, actually. After services the Caravan's going to take off to Tennessee and get a farm. Because what you put your attention into you get more of, and I need more trees, more grass, more wheat, more soybeans, more healthy babies, more good-looking sane people, people that can work. That's what I really want to see a lot more of and that's what I'm going to put my attention into. That's why I want to go out and really get into it with the dirt—put attention into that and manifest a bunch of that.

Okay, are we all up to karmic zero for where we're at right now? Let's see the horn, I'd like to start it out with the horn. God Bless you all. Thank you very much for coming here. I really love you a lot. I just love you a whole bunch, and we'll see you whenever we see you, down whatever road we go down.

God Bless you and good morning.

*Well, after we got to San Francisco and got the Caravan parked in a safe space, we then had one more piece of business to do: We had to go up to Grants Pass and turn ourselves in to the judge. It was kind of funny going up to Grants Pass, just going through that territory now that we knew what went on there . And we came into the office, and it was a gas. Every empty space of wall in that district attorney's whole office was filled up with newspaper clippings about the Caravan going through towns all across the United States and what we said to people in those towns, and the guys treated us like returning heroes. And the judge had us come into the courtroom, and he said, "Well, you did a good job out there, and your presence here in the courtroom is an embarrassment. You guys are free to go."*

*And that was the real end of the Caravan.*

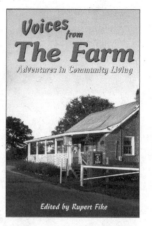

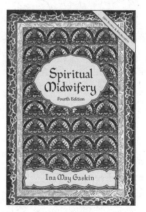